HOW TO RIDE YOUR HOBBY

BY FREDERICK A. COLLINS

What do you collect? Is it stamps, marbles, autographs, leaves, shells, or pictures of aircraft? Maybe you don't collect things, maybe you build things or raise a garden or play some musical instrument. But there is surely something that you do "just for the fun of it."

There are hundreds of different hobbies, and some of them require real skill. In this book you will not only find a list of all these hobbies but also some practical information about each one of them. It tells you exactly how to start any particular collection, what materials you need, what it costs, what you must look for, where to get things for your collection, and anything else you should know in order to get the most pleasure from your hobby.

There are dozens of fascinating hobbies besides that of collecting. You can make yourself the most popular member of your crowd by learning palmistry, astrology, graphology, or some other from of fortune-telling. Or you can learn to entertain your friends with tricks of magic or with silhouettes or hat impersonations. Scientific hobbies can be useful as well as entertaining. Radio, television, homemade phonograph records, and weather forecasting are only a few of the fields that will challenge your cleverness and hold your interest. Making models is also lots of fun, and this book gives you information about making model houses, ships, stagecoaches, yachts, and many kinds of aircraft.

The hobbies described here are all so fascinating that you may want to take up several of them. It is better, though, to start with one and concentrate all your efforts on it. Later you can take up a second hobby, one that is quite different from your first.

* * * * * * *

HOW TO RIDE YOUR HOBBY

HOW TO RIDE
YOUR HOBBY

By

A. FREDERICK COLLINS, F.R.A.S.

Illustrated

This special edition is published by arrangement
with the publisher of the regular edition,
D. Appleton-Century Company.

CADMUS BOOKS
E. M. HALE AND COMPANY
Chicago

J
790
Collins

To

my young friend

JEANETTE ALEXANDER STEVENS

The Girl of a Hundred Hobbies

A WORD TO YOU

Dang the mon that invinted work by
the dizzy light of a candle; dang the
mon that invinted work a-tol, a-tol.

OLD IRISH SAYING

WHAT we call *work* is anything that we must do and that
we don't like to do, and what we call *recreation* is anything that we don't have to do but which we like to do
more than anything else, and do it whenever we get a
chance. It then automatically becomes a *hobby,* and when
it does so we get the utmost pleasure out of it, and this is
really living.

Now work as performed by mankind means the exertion
of the mental faculties or of the physical body, or both of
these combined, for the particular purpose of accomplish-
ing something. It is, therefore, work that is responsible
for the relative progress of the arts, the sciences, and the
industries, and, it follows, the advancement of our material and social well being. From this you will gather
that work is a vital factor in our lives and today it is the
watchword of the world, but more especially here in the
United States, where we strive to achieve in the shortest
possible time, and in so doing we burn the electric light
at both ends.

Since the above premises are admitted, it should follow
that the man who is achieving things by work of whatever

kind would get the greatest pleasure out of doing so, and he would if it were not for certain odious conditions that are imposed upon him and which keep him in a constant state of worry and give him nerve fag. Named, these conditions are (1) sustained effort, (2) long hours, (3) confinement, (4) subjugation, and (5) poor wages.

Without going into a detailed description of these various factors, it will be enough to say here that separately or together they produce both mental and physical *fatigue,* and it is this that irks the worker and makes him long for the life of his primordial ancestor whose only worry was the preservation of his own hide.

The common definition of *fatigue* is the loss of strength and endurance, while the physiological definition goes a shade farther by saying it is a condition of the cells and organs which have undergone functional activity. The result of this reaction is a decrease of the energy-holding compounds that are available for work and the accumulation of poisonous waste matters.

Assuming that the above theory of fatigue fits the facts in the case, in order to build up the source of power and remove the waste products the logical thing to do is to stop work and so shut off the disagreeable conditions. As this utopian scheme is seldom practicable, there is another way by which you can in a large measure circumvent them, and so recover your strength; this is to take up some form of recreation, i. e., *to ride a hobby* of some kind, and you will find dozens of them explained in this book.

Curiously enough, when you ride a hobby you may expend the same amount of mental or physical energy, or both, as you do when you are working, but there is this great difference between them, to wit, in the first you are removed from the conditions which make work odious; thus you can (*a*) relax when and as often as you wish, (*b*) put in as much or as little time as you want to, (*c*) you are not confined against your will, (*d*) you are not doing it for the sake of the almighty dollar, and (*e*) you are not irked by the injustice of the little you get for the amount of work you have to do. It is the lack of the first-named restraining conditions that adds to the pleasure which your skill and other attributes give you when you ride a hobby.

So, brother, let me whisper in your ear that whatever kind of work you may be doing, you should by all means get yourself a hobby and ride the rough edges off of your work, to the end that you may retain your health, your youth, your interest, and your sense of humor, and so when you reach the three-quarter stretch you will come bounding home and be declared a winner in Life's great sweepstake.

A. FREDERICK COLLINS

Island Park, L. I.
New York

CONTENTS

CONTENTS

HOW TO RIDE YOUR HOBBY

CHAPTER I

ABOUT OWNING A HOBBY

YES, a *hobby* is the kind of a nag you want to ride, and as I have been in the business of training and riding 'em all my life, it gives me the greatest pleasure to tell you how to break one in and go galloping over Elysian fields and away on it. But first off, let's find out just what manner of beastie the hobby is.

How the Hobby Got Its Name.—In the glamorous old days of Merrie England when Geoffrey Chaucer, the Father of English poetry, was writing his magic verse, a horse was often called a *hobbyn,* and as time moved on apace and the language was improved, this was changed to *hobby.*

The *morris dance* was a great favorite in those pristine times and it was executed in pageants, pantomimes, at festivals, and the like. The dancers wore the fancy costumes of Robin Hood, Maid Marian and other legendary characters, and there was always one of them who essayed the rôle of the *hobby-horse.* This *animule* consisted of a small dummy figure of a horse through whose body was a large hole; the performer slipped this figure over his own body and fastened it to his waist.

As he pranced and cavorted around he was apparently riding the horse but, as a matter of precise statement, the horse was riding him, all of which provided no end of merriment. From the antics of this burlesque *horsey*

1

came the colloquial expression *riding a hobby,* which has come to mean the act of pursuing some object without apparently achieving any useful purpose. To us ultra-moderns, a *hobby* is anything we like to do to the exclusion of all other things, that is to *ride it,* and from which we do not look for a reward of any kind, except that of unalloyed pleasure and its concomitants of enjoyment and gratification.

Why You Should Have a Hobby.—The trite saying that "all work and no play makes Jack a dull boy" states the case for the hobby in a nutshell. To have to sweat all of your waking hours to keep the wolf from the door or, worse still, to hoard up wealth for its own sake, is to live a wormlike, two-dimensional existence, and, hence, it were better not to have lived at all.

Most of us, however, emulate the caterpillar, in that we start out laboriously by crawling along the rocky road of life, with only one objective in view, and that is the pursuit and capture of food. Then the caterpillar wraps a cocoon around itself, and we wrap ourselves around a hobby; comes a brief resting period when we, like it, emerge with scintillating wings into the bright sunshine of a new and glorified world, and flit about in the other dimension, i. e., height, with the ecstatic joy of living.

Soaring in four dimensions, or *space-time* as the relativists call it, now and then a little while every day, free from dull care, anxious worries and hard work, gives you not only a broader vision concerning the realities of life, but it serves the noble purpose of taking the rough edges off of the sordid side of it; and when you do this, the act of living becomes a really worth while performance.

To have a hobby that you can ride with intensive interest and inflated enthusiasm has many things to commend it besides those which we consider the primary by-products of it, namely, pleasure, enjoyment and gratification. Among the secondary values are that it clears away the cobwebs of your brain spun by the routine work you are doing, which is your vocation and by which you live; this in turn relieves to a large extent the strain on your nervous system, with the result that this greatly helps to keep you physically fit.

The above statements being true, it follows as the night the day, that a hobby is one of the brightest things you can have in your young lexicon of life, for it heads off mental depression, gives you physical poise and makes you an interesting person wherever you and a few of the intelligentsia may foregather. The reason you will become imbued with these excellent characteristics is because your great interest and unbounded enthusiasm gives you an approximate superiority complex that those you meet will appreciate and be bound to take cognizance of.

It is sadly true that you will occasionally find a hobbyist who has been so badly bitten by the bug that he repeats, *ad infinitum,* the catechism of his pet avocation, in and out of season, until his friends may, like the boarder whose landlady served him with beans for forty or fifty straight luncheons, get just a leetle tired. But even when they are bored to extinction with his repetitious recitals concerning the thing he most dearly loves, they still respect his sincerity and earnestness and, withal, his good intentions.

And now let's find out what the chief hobbies are and, assuming you haven't any, the particular one that will be the most likely to take you for the best ride.

The Various Kinds of Hobbies.—Since anything that you are passionately fond of doing, and which you do whenever you have the spare time, and sometimes when you haven't, constitutes a hobby, it would be manifestly impossible for me to tell you all about the various ones in this book, but what I shall do is to give you an outline of those that are the most important, or popular, or both, to the end that you may select the one which will meet your particular requirements to the best advantage.

Now there are three general kinds of hobbies, and these are (*1*) the mental, or psychical, (*2*) the body, or physical, and (*3*) a combination of these two, or the psycho-physical. The *mental*, or *psychical* hobbies are those that require the exercise of your thinking apparatus only, such as solving puzzles, playing games of various kinds, collecting stamps and other things, travel, etc.

The *body*, or *physical* hobbies are those in which you must needs call into play chiefly the action of your muscles, such as athletics and sports, as for example, walking, climbing, running, jumping, swimming, riding, and the like. The *psycho-physical* hobbies are those in which your mind and hand must be coördinated and do team work in order to produce the results you want; wood and metal working and making things in general, as well as many of the scientific hobbies are of this nature.

The above generalized classification will give you an inkling of what the various hobbies are. I shall not, however, go into the matter of puzzles, games, athletics or sports in this book, since all of them are so well known they need not be included here. Instead, I shall tell you about the hobbies that you can take up which come more within the meaning of the word.

The Kind of a Hobby You Need.—Many folks of my acquaintance got started on their especial hobbies in a more or less accidental way, and without giving them the slightest forethought. If you happen to do likewise, you may possibly stumble onto one that will serve you nobly and well. However, if the hobby you choose happens to require an initial outlay to start with and a constant expenditure to keep it going, you may find you have a white elephant on your hands. By giving the matter a little previous consideration you may find something that is better suited to your needs and save yourself no small amount of grief.

Now there are at least five prime conditions that a hobby must satisfy if you are to ride it to a successful finish: it must (1) strongly appeal to you, (2) be suited to your age, (3) fit in with the time you can give it, (4) be adaptable to your ability, and (5) line up with your pocketbook.

Generally speaking, the kind of a hobby you ought to take up should be quite different from the work you do; thus, if you are a teacher, a bookkeeper, or are engaged in any vocation that is chiefly mental, you should choose some hobby that calls for physical exercise, such as gardening and other out-of-door occupations. On the other hand, if your vocation is one of physical labor, then some mental hobby such as making a collection, one of the fine arts, playing a musical instrument, giving entertainments, or following some scientific pursuit, is the best kind for you to indulge in.

Many people, especially those of the male persuasion,

just naturally run to the use of wood- and metal-working tools, and so some one of the manual arts makes a hobby that fits them like a glove. Femininity takes to the fine arts even as a duckling takes to water. Boys and girls and men and women, whether their regular work is of a mental or a physical nature, like, as a rule, animal and plant hobbies; this is perfectly natural, for it was in these avocations that the human race was first interested, and it cannot be gainsaid but that living creatures are far more interesting than non-living objects.

Children should have their hobbies as well as the grown-ups. Little boys are keen on collecting small things such as marbles, and I know an eight-year-old who has a mighty interesting collection of pebbles, and his father is teaching him how to polish them. Another boy friend of mine specializes in shells. Little boys are very partial to mechanical things and especially to toy railroad trains. Little girls like their little brothers' hobbies too, but their main forte is collecting dolls and toys, drawing and painting, and many of them play musical instruments, from the jew's-harp to the piano.

About 90 per cent, I should say, of the older boys and younger men like mechanical, electrical and chemical hobbies, and these should be encouraged, for the efforts they put forth bring not only the transitory emolument of pleasure, but the lasting benefits which result from training the mind to think in terms of accuracy and continuity. Finally, there is no finer hobby than travel, and this holds good for all ages, beginning with youth, but it is especially suited to those of mature years, provided, of course, they have the wherewithal to manage it.

Usually, when one has the urge to take up a given

hobby, he will ordinarily have the mental and physical ability to cope with it. If the hobby he chooses requires some degree of mental or manipulative skill, as in the case of the fine arts, manual arts, playing musical instruments, making scientific experiments, etc., the hobbyist who is not innately gifted along the line he has taken up will find the results he obtains far from gratifying and his hobby will speedily degenerate into something very like a headache.

What Your Hobby Will Cost.—Almost any kind of a hobby that you go in for will cost you money—a little or a lot depending on what it is and the thoroughness with which you ride it. So before you definitely choose one you should give the monetary end of it some little consideration.

As an illustration of what your hobby can cost you, take the making of a stamp collection; the outlay may range from next to nothing to the sky as the limit. Thus a beginner's stamp collection need not cost you anything, but one like that owned by King George, of Great Britain, is said to be worth *$50,000*. Autographs of your friends can be had without price, except for the book they are written in, but those of noted men and women run up into some pretty high figures.

A collection of present-day coins of this and other countries can be had at their face value, but certain older coins are worth many times their weight in gold. If your hobby is dogs or cats you will not have to pay very much for them if they are of mongrel breed, but if they are thoroughbreds your pocketbook will shrink quite perceptibly. All animals of a smaller kind are comparatively cheap and make the finest of hobbies.

Gardening and other plant hobbies are, as a rule, quite inexpensive, but if you want to specialize in orchids and other rare and exotic specimens of plant life, then you must expect to pay for them.

Your chief outlay for a manual arts hobby will be for tools and materials. Hand wood-working tools cost comparatively little, a power scroll saw is far from being expensive, while a lathe for doing metal work will pull perceptibly on your purse strings, that is, if you get a good one. Experimenting with radio is a delightful hobby and one that you can afford to indulge in; especially is this true if you care to strain a point and make a little money out of it, and this also applies to the building of model ships, airplanes, etc.

The hobbies that are classified as fine arts also call for a minimum outlay except where certain kinds of photography are indulged in. As you know an ordinary camera can be had for a few dollars, but where you are making it your hobby, you should have a much better equipment. If your hobby is taking motion pictures and projecting them, then you must be prepared to spend your *roll* like a jockey who has won his golden spurs.

Of course, you know about what musical instruments of different kinds cost. If your hobby is playing a harmonica, your initial expense will be something less than a dollar; if it is a saxophone your exchequer will be set back to the tune of from *$60.00* to *$600.00,* while a piano accordion will cost you from *$100.00* to *$500.00.* But my earnest suggestion is that you love thy neighbor as thyself and save your money by taking up some noiseless and, it follows, painless, hobby.

A very excellent one that will not only give you a lot of fun and pleasure and make your neighbor love you even as he loves himself is ventriloquism, sleight-of-hand, or some of the other various branches of entertainment. The monetary requirement is very little for any of these acts but you will have to pay handsomely for them in time and patience, for in order to give a performance that is at all satisfactory you have got to be good, that's all.

Scientific hobbies usually run into something that looks like real money but, to my way of thinking, they pay the biggest dividends in the long run, for while you profit in temporary pleasure you also gain by permanently improving your mind. If you are interested in electricity, microscopy, or astronomy, you can cut down the initial expense very considerably by making the needed apparatus and instruments yourself, and doing these things are most fascinating hobbies in themselves.

By all odds the finest hobby you can have is *travel*, for it is the great eye-opener, brain-stimulator and mind-awakener. To ride it so that you will get the greatest pleasure out of it you must needs have a good-sized drawing account in some perfectly solvent bank so that wherever you go you will be in funds. Personally, my hobby is travel—I love it above all other things—and I am never so happy as when I am miserable traveling second-class in some foreign country.

When a Hobby Becomes a Business.—In the sporting world you are an *amateur* when you play the game for the sheer love of it, and a *professional* when you play it for the money there is in it. In the earlier part of this chapter I intimated that you lose your standing as a hobbyist when you make money out of your hobby and you then become just a plain, ordinary business person.

There are, however, a large number of businesses that had their origins in hobbies. That is to say, a person will take up some hobby for the pure love of it, and without the slightest idea or intention of getting any pecuniary benefit from it, and without any effort on his or her part it becomes a paying proposition. There is no valid reason why if your hobby breaks that way for you, you shouldn't cash in on it if you care to do so.

Here are a few instances of where a hobby was productive of pleasure but resulted in material emoluments as well. Professor S. W. Burnham, of Chicago, was a court stenographer by profession. He became interested in astronomy as a hobby and built his own telescope. He started in by discovering double stars with it and finally became one of the greatest astronomers of his time. He picked out the site for the Lick Observatory, on Mount Hamilton, California, and became the senior astronomer there. Later on he was connected with the Yerkes Observatory, at Williams Bay, Wisconsin, and was the professor of practical astronomy at the University of Chicago.

Henry Ford, of Dearborn, Michigan, was a machinist by trade and his hobby was making things. He conceived the idea of building a gasoline buggy, or motor car as it is now called, just as a hobby, but it worked so well, he was prevailed upon by his friends to build like cars for them. He finally went into the business of manufacturing and marketing them—and how!

Dr. Raymond L. Ditmars was in his youth a reporter

on the New York *World*. His hobby was to hobnob with snakes! Great snakes! And so great was his interest in them he always carried a few in a bag around with him. He became the foremost authority on *herpetology*, which is that branch of zoölogy that has to do with the structure, classification and habits of reptiles.

He is now Curator of Reptiles of the New York Zoological Garden and he has recently returned from Trinidad, a small, rocky, volcanic island of the British West Indies, whence he went to and secured a specimen of the *bushmaster*, a very rare, elusive and venomous snake. Land snakes!

CHAPTER II

SOME COLLECTING HOBBIES

PART I

STAMP AND COIN COLLECTING

FROM the hobbyist's point of view a *collection* is an aggregation—that is the bringing together—of a number of items or objects and making a display of them. From this premise it follows that a collection can be made of almost all related or unrelated things, the only condition which must be satisfied is that each separate piece shall be portable and placed in proximity with the others.

To show the great difference in the scope of collections, there is on the one hand the simple, costless, and withal pretty one that little Ikey has made of cigar-bands, and, on the other, the complex, expensive and gorgeous one that King Solomon made of some *800* wives. I would not, however, have you emulate the small boy of today or the wise old man of long ago, but rather I would like to see you make a collection that is betwixt and between these two extremes.

The collections which I have described in this chapter will give you a very good idea of some of the most important ones that you can make at a minimum cost, are highly edifying, and from which you can choose a hobby

12

that you can ride to your heart's content, and you need not be afraid of getting bucked off.

The Philatelic or Stamp Collecting Hobby.—From the time the postage stamp was invented nearly a hundred years ago, *philately*,[1] or the collecting of them, has been a favorite indoor hobby, and it is far and away the most popular one that is ridden today. There are many reasons why it has not only survived since its inception but has also grown to gigantic proportions in the intervening years. Among the obvious ones are that stamps are (*1*) easily had, (*2*) they cost anywhere from absolute zero to a king's ransom, (*3*) they are compact and easily handled, (*4*) they are miniature works of art, (*5*) they are educational, being biographical, geographical and historical, (*6*) new and commemorative stamps are constantly being issued, and (*7*) searching for old and valuable ones is like prospecting for gold—a lifelong joy.

Why You Should Collect Stamps.—To make a collection of stamps you must pay particular attention to their arrangement in your album, and this will help you to be neat and to develop method and order. By studying each stamp in your collection, you will become accurate in your observations, quick in deductions and keen-witted to a high degree. When you have once started on your hobby you will get the greatest pleasure out of talking and trading stamps with other eager and ardent fans like

---

[1] In classical language the study and collecting of postage stamps, stamped envelops, etc., is called *philately* (pronounced phi-*lat'*-e-ly) ; one who collects and makes a study of them is called a *philatelist* (pronounced phi-*lat'*-e-list), while anything that pertains to philately is called *philatelic* (pronounced phil-a-*tel'*-ic), and be sure to pronounce these words right. All of them are derived from the Greek combining form *philos* which means *loving*, and the noun *telos* meaning *free from tax*, i.e., a *postage stamp*, hence, *loving postage stamps*.

yourself; and of all the ways to make your spare time fly, one of the best is to sort out freshly acquired stamps and mount them in your album.

How to Start a Stamp Collection.—When you get a letter with a one-cent Benjamin Franklin, or a two- or a three-cent George Washington stamp on it you are not very much impressed because it is so familiar you are scarcely conscious that it is there. But when you get a letter with a newly issued, a commemorative, an air-mail, or a foreign stamp on it, you are very apt to take a good look at it and even if you are not a collector, go so far as to remove and save it.

Very often this is the impulse that you obey to start a stamp collection and from that time on you will be on the still-hunt for others which are new and novel. When you have garnered a few you may get a blank-book of some kind, rule it off into squares, and begin to paste them in it. While this way of starting will lead you on toward the goal of a real collection, it is a long road and a rather tedious ride.

The easier, quicker and far more pleasurable way to start a stamp collection is to buy an album that is made especially for the purpose, and which you can get of any dealer in stamps. An album that will serve your needs if you are a beginner can be had for as little as *50* cents. The next step is to buy a packet that contains *1,000* foreign stamps which will cost you *$1.00* or less.

A still better scheme is to get what is known as *The Imperial Stamp Collecting Outfit* (see *Fig. 1*), as this provides everything that you need to start a stamp collection. It includes an album, *300* different foreign stamps, *1,000* stamp hinges, a millimeter scale and perforation gauge, and a booklet called *The Standard Guide to Stamp Collecting*. This latter explains step by step the things which you, as an embryo collector, should do and know. The price of this outfit complete is only *$1.00*.

A very much better beginner's outfit is one that contains either *125* different United States stamps, or *1,000* different foreign stamps; a nineteenth-century set of coats-of-arms, the rulers and the merchant flags of all of

FIG. 1.—THE IMPERIAL STAMP COLLECTING OUTFIT

the countries of the world; also a pair of stamp tongs, a perforation gauge and a watermark detector. The complete outfit can be had for the small sum of *$2.50*.[2]

In the course of time you will find that you have a number of duplicate stamps on hand, and these are useful to trade for others that you haven't got. To preserve and classify these duplicates and make it safe to carry them in your pocket you can get stock cards and stock

[2] You can get this and all other stamp supplies from the Scott Stamp and Coin Company, *1* West *47*th Street, New York City.

books. The *stock cards* have linen strips on them which form pockets as shown at *A* in *Fig. 2,* and the stock books consist of a number of stock cards bound between covers as at *B*.

The Tools You Need.—Stamps are easily damaged, and therefore they should be handled just as little as

A — A STOCK CARD   (*Pocket Size*)

B — A STOCK BOOK   (*Pocket Size*)

FIG. 2.—HOW TO CARRY YOUR STAMPS SAFELY

possible. When you must handle them you should use, not your fingers, but a pair of little tweezers, called *stamp tongs* which are shown at *A* in *Fig. 3*. Another thing, stamps should never be mounted directly on the page of your album but to a *stamp hinge* and this, in turn, on the page.

The study of stamps is not confined to the designs on them alone but extends to the perforations and watermarks. The *perforations,* or just *perfs,* as they are called for short, are the minute holes that are punched in a line between and around the stamps. The sizes and shapes of the holes varies as well as the distance between them; very often it is by means of them that the collector can tell a stamp of little value from one of great value. The

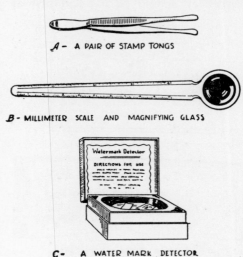

A - A PAIR OF STAMP TONGS

B - MILLIMETER SCALE AND MAGNIFYING GLASS

C - A WATER MARK DETECTOR

FIG. 3.—THE TOOLS YOU NEED FOR STAMP COLLECTING

different kinds of perforations are shown in the *Standard Stamp Catalogue.*

To measure the perforations, a small rule called a *millimeter scale* or a *perforation gauge* is used. You can get one engraved on heavy Bristol board for *10* cents postpaid, or one made of metal with a magnifying glass mounted on the end of it, see *B,* and packed in a plush-lined box for *$1.00,* postage extra.

A *watermark* is a design produced by the pressure of

a roller with a raised figure on it against the paper when it is being made. The paper becomes thinner where the figure presses on it, and in ordinary paper the watermark can be seen by holding it up to the light. The watermark in paper that stamps are printed on cannot be seen so easily because the ink impression on it is opaque.

To see the watermark on a stamp you must use a *watermark detector*, see *C*, and this is a small tray made of black glass or other substance. Some benzine or carbon tetrachloride is poured into the tray and the stamp is immersed in it, when the watermarks will stand out in black lines. The watermark does not in any way affect the value of the stamp, but it does enable you to tell a genuine from a counterfeit one. A black crystalline tray will reveal the most obscure watermarks and you can get one for *50* cents. The different kinds of watermarks are shown in the *Standard Stamp Catalogue*.

When You Have Made Your Start.—You will find that as soon as you have your stamp collection well under way, you will strike up an acquaintance with other collectors in your neighborhood; in nearly every city there is one or more stamp collectors' clubs [3] and you should join one of them, for making contact with those who are veterans in the saddle will give you a liberal education in riding your new hobby.

Another and important means by which you can increase your knowledge of stamps is to subscribe for a paper that is devoted to the subject, two of which are

[3] If you live in New York City you can join The Collectors Club Inc., *30* East *42*nd St. It meets two evenings a week at *8* o'clock and holds lectures, exhibitions, auction sales and exchanges. It publishes a magazine called the *Philatelist*.

Stamps,[4] and *Scott's Monthly Journal.*[5] Finally you will quickly come to a point where you will have great need for a *Standard Stamp Catalogue,* which is the stamp collector's *Bible.* This book contains a picture, gives a description and tells the price of every postage stamp that has ever been issued by all of the various governments of the world.

Each stamp in it is numbered and, hence, when either a stamp or its number is cited, you will be able to quickly learn all about it. To keep up with the issues of new stamps, a new edition of the *Catalogue,* that is brought right up-to-date, is published every year. In this country *Scott's* is the standard catalogue and the price of it is *$2.50.* You need not buy one, however, if you live in a city, for every public library has a copy of it or, at least, should have one.

The Numismatic or Coin Collecting Hobby.—The hobby of collecting coins, or *numismatics,*[6] to give it its high-toned name, runs a close second to that of collecting stamps. As a matter of truth and equable justice, the former is a far more well-bred hobby than the latter, and it's a safe bet that it would be a nose ahead of it but for the fact that it costs something more to start a collection and to build it up; moreover, coins are bulkier than stamps and, it follows, they take up considerably more room.

There are numerous reasons, however, why many col-

[4] This is published by The Collectors Club Inc., 30 East 43rd St.

[5] This is published by the Scott Stamp and Coin Company.

[6] We get the name *numismatics* (pronounced nu-miz-*mat'*-iks), which means the *science of coins,* and *numismatist* (pronounced nu-*miz'*-ma-tist), which means an *expert in coins,* or a *collector of coins,* from the Latin word *nomisma,* meaning a *piece of money,* or a *coin.*

lectors choose to make coins their hobby rather than stamps, and the chief ones are because (*1*) while stamps have no inherent value, since the paper they are printed on is worth nothing, coins always have a face value and they are, naturally, worth their weight in whatever metal they are made of; (*2*) whereas stamps are of comparatively recent invention, coins have been in use for *2,700* years, and handling a bit of paper that is less than *100* years old does not begin to stir the imagination as does a coin of ancient lineage; and, finally, (*3*) stamps, as you know, are easily destroyed, while coins outlast the elements, and even time itself. These, then, are a few of the reasons why thousands of collectors are riding the hobby of coins for dear life and getting the keenest pleasure out of it.

Why You Should Collect Coins.—By collecting coins, even haphazardly, you will get enough pleasure and gratification out of it to make you love it as a hobby; you will, at the same time, learn a lot about things that come under the head of useful information as, for example, the alloys they are made of, how they are made, about their weights, comparative values, etc.

But to be a real collector of coins you must go much deeper into their meaning, and to do this you must like the subjects of history, mythology, archeology, government, customs, costumes, and other things that have to do with races which have long since vanished from the earth. Indeed, much of what is known of them at the present time has been deciphered by collectors who have made an intensive study of their coins.

If you will make a collection of early Greek and Roman coins with these considerations in mind, you will be .

fascinated with your hobby and carried along by it with an earnestness and enthusiasm that will surprise you and your friends as well; for it is then that all of your mental faculties will be called into play and these will aid and abet your imagination, develop your taste for the beautiful, improve your picturesque characteristics, and add mightily to your powers of understanding.

How to Start a Coin Collection.—The desire to start a collection of coins originates in various ways as, for example, (*1*) reading about the delight and value of doing so, (*2*) coming into possession of some curious or ancient coin, (*3*) knowing some one who is collecting them, and (*4*) being given a collection of them.

To build up a collection of coins of the world is not as easy and costs considerably more than to build up a like collection of stamps, and for this reason it is a good scheme to specialize in a given series. Thus you can start with small or large pennies, or with *2, 3, 5, 10, 25* or *50* cent pieces, or the *$1.00* coins of the United States.

Your first key coin which is to form the nucleus of your collection can be of any date, and then by looking at every coin you get of the same series, you will be able to gradually add those of an earlier or a later date until you have one for every year that they were minted. In following this course, you will eventually need coins of certain dates that are quite scarce and, it follows, some of them will be hard to get at any price.[7]

[7] The *1804* dollar is one of them, and this is a fake because there were no silver dollars minted by the government in that year. But in *1837* a former mint worker made about a dozen of them, and foolish collectors paid as high as *$2000.00* a piece for them. A real buy, however, is the *Fugio* dollar designed by our own Benjamin Franklin which was minted in *1776*. On the obverse side is a sundial and the motto *Mind Your Busi-*

Instead of building up a collection of series date coins, that is by getting a coin of a given kind for every year beginning with the first one that was minted until they were no longer minted—and of which you are pretty sure to become tired as soon, and often before, you have it completed—you will find it much more interesting to make a collection of *Colonial* and *Continental American* coins, as these have a fine old patriotic and historic background.

A hobby fit for a king and one which is largely in vogue among the remaining royal families of Europe is collecting ancient coins. The earliest known coin is the *Ægina stater* [8] which was made of *electrum,* a natural alloy containing about 27 per cent of silver and 73 per cent gold. It was minted in Ægina, a Greek island in the Gulf of Ægina, about the year 700 B. C. A large number of this coin has been found and you can get one for about $5.00. The earliest known gold coin is the Crœsus, and this was minted in Lydia in the sixth century B. C., and you can get one for $10.00.

You can make a highly interesting collection of coins by beginning with the *Ægina stater* and following on with one for every 50 years thereafter up to 1630. If you will be satisfied with coins that are fairly well preserved you can get a collection of them for about $25.00, but if you feel that they must be in perfect condition, then they will cost you in the neighborhood of twice the above amount.

Price Lists and Catalogues.—The first thing you should

---

ness, while on the reverse side is a chain formed of links with the name of the state that issued it and the legend *American Congress. We Are One.*

[8] From the Greek word *stater* which means *coin.*

have if you are going to make coin collecting a real hobby
is a price list or a catalogue of coins. There are several
different ones published and chief among these are:

1. *The Standard Price List of United States Coins.*
This lists and shows pictures of all the more obtainable
early American coins, all of the kinds of United States
silver and copper coins, and quotes the price at which
most of them can be bought. This is a very good guide for
the amateur collector and only costs 25 cents.[9]

2. *A Standard Premium List of Rare United States and
Early American Coins* is a beautifully illustrated booklet
with over 200 reproductions of the rareties in the United
States Series, the private issues of gold coins of a number
of states, and the early coins of the Colonies, beginning
with the *pine tree shilling* and *hog money* of Bermuda.
There is also a supplement that lists the rare United States
notes and other paper money. This is a very useful reference book for collectors, libraries and banking houses.
Its price is likewise 25 cents.

3. *The Standard Catalogue of United States Coins and
Currency* lists and describes all the United States coins
and currency and gives the prices at which most of them
may be purchased. It includes early American coins from
1652 to *1796;* all of the United States gold, silver and
copper coins; private gold issues from *1830* to *1861;*
commemorative coins; early Colonial and Continental
notes; United States notes; fractional currency, and Con-
federate and Southern States notes. You can get a copy
of it for *$2.50.*

How to Keep Your Coins.—There are two chief ways
for you to keep your coins so that they are easily labeled,

[9] This is published by the Scott Stamp and Coin Company.

classified and examined, and these are (*1*) in coin boxes and (*2*) in coin albums. The *coin boxes* are beautifully made of pasteboard covered with black paper, with a raised label in one end for the general record of the coin, and a flat label on the back for a more detailed description of it. These are the kind of boxes that are used by numismatic museums and coin hobbyists to display their collections. You can get a complete set of *13* sample boxes of different sizes, from a little one that will hold a gold dollar to a large one for a *3*-inch medal for *25* cents of J. James Clarke, *39* Charles Street, Jamestown, New York.

The *coin album* consists of individual pages, each of which is about ⅛ of an inch thick, 7½ inches wide and *14* inches long, and in this are little circular windows the size of which corresponds to the diameter of the coins you want to display, as is shown at *A* in *Fig. 4.* The windows are made of transparent celluloid strips and these cover the coins on both sides so that the obverse and reverse surfaces can be seen. The celluloid strips can be easily slipped into and out of the page with your fingers, so that you can quickly remove any coin you may want to examine. Each of these pages costs *$1.00* and five of them can be put into a *coin album binder,* see *B,* which will cost you an additional *$2.00.*

Papers and Societies.—You should by all means subscribe to one of the periodicals that is devoted to the interests of coin collectors, and two good ones are *The Coin Collector's Journal* and *The Numismatist.* The first named is published by the Scott Stamp and Coin Company, *1* West *47*th Street, New York City, and the second

by the American Numismatic Association, *4215* Fernhill
Avenue, Baltimore, Maryland.

If you live here in New York, or come here, be sure to
visit the *American Numismatic Society* at *156*th Street
and Broadway. You will find here the finest collection of

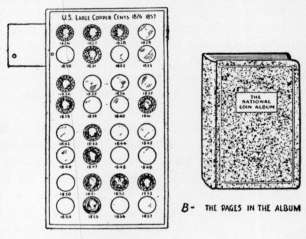

A - ONE OF THE COIN PAGES

B - THE PAGES IN THE ALBUM

FIG. 4.—THE NATIONAL COIN ALBUM

coins in the United States and—glory be—there is no
admission charged. Connoisseurs are here ready to give
you expert advice about anything you may want to know
that has to do with coins, medals or paper money, and it
is all free for the asking.

If you are sufficiently interested in coins, you should
join the American Numismatic Society, for many advantages will accrue to you if you do so. Among these are
the resources of a very complete and effectively classified

library where you can work under the best possible conditions.

A series of *Numismatic Notes and Monographs* are published by the Society and sent to its members without any additional charge. There are now more than *60* of these monographs and from four to six are issued annually, all of them by the leading authorities on coins and allied subjects. You can become an *Associate Member* of the Society for *$5.00* a year, or a *Fellow* for *$10.00* a year.

PART II

SOME OTHER COLLECTING HOBBIES

Collecting Autographs and Autographed Books.— An *autograph* is, as you probably know, one's own *signature,* or *handwriting.* Now, one of the most painless, enduring, and, above all, personal hobbies that you can ride is that of collecting autographs. In my boyhood days nearly every man, woman and child had an autograph album, and in it were the inscriptions of father, mother, and other members of the family, the relatives, the pastor, the teacher, the dear friends, and last and most prized of all, was the one of the boy or girl sweetheart.

Then every once in a while a celebrity would happen along—say some noted evangelist, lecturer, author, actor or singer, to say nothing of the silver-tongued political orator—and when the collector would succeed in getting his or her name in his book, what a wonderful thrill it gave him, and one that he remembered with unalloyed pleasure whenever he chanced to gaze at the album, espe-

cially in after years. A few signatures of famous personages are shown in *Fig. 5*.[10]

To make your collection of autographs of greater interest than the mere inscriptions offer, you can take up
graphology, which is the *study of handwriting*, and is
supposed to enable you to judge the person's character,
disposition and aptitude for certain things. There are

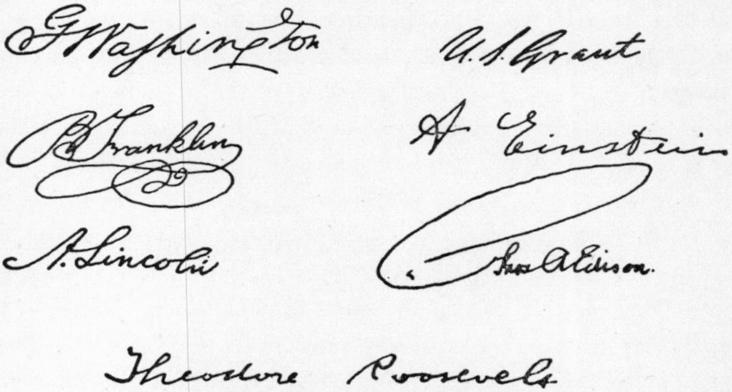

FIG. 5.—AUTOGRAPHS OF FAMOUS MEN

numerous books to be had on the subject,[11] any one of
which will give you the alleged principles of it, but do
not, by any means, be misled into the belief that it is at
all scientific or that there is anything really in it. But you
will get a lot of fun out of analyzing the autographs that
you collect and you can further enhance the sentimental
value of them by keeping the record of your deductions
along with those of the signatures.

[10] You can buy autographs, rare books and old documents, of the Hoag
Book Company, Box 9, Pratt Station, Brooklyn, N. Y.

[11] A couple of good books on *graphology* are *Handwriting and Character*, by Dewitt B. Lucas, published by David McKay, Philadelphia,
and *Psychology of Handwriting*, by William French, published by
G. P. Putnam's Sons, New York City.

Collecting Autographed Books.—This is one of the most useful, satisfying and lasting of all of the hobbies that come under the head of *making collections,* and yet it is one that is not at the present time practised to any great extent. But my observations lead me to believe that it is gradually gaining momentum and should grow rapidly in popular favor.

The idea is this: Every time you buy a book, have it suitably inscribed *by the author* of it. Thus you not only make a collection of autographs of the men and women who wrote the books but, and this is of greater importance, you build up a library at the same time.

The way to go about it is simple, for all you have to do is to buy the books you want, one at a time, when the spirit moves you, then write to the author of it and ask him if he will be so kind and condescending as to autograph it for you, if you will send it on to him. Unless he has a chronic case of indigestion, or other ailment of a grouchy nature, he will be so proud and delighted with the honor of your request that he will hasten to assure you that the pleasure will be all his own. He will also ask that you send the aforesaid book to him by return post *prepaid,* and not to forget to send enough stamps to pay the postage back on it.

When you write to the author send your letter to him in care of the publishers of his books, for publishers make it a rule not to give the address of an author to any one who may ask for it, but they will forward a letter to him that is sent in their care.

Collecting Articles, Newspapers and Pictures.— Collecting articles, or *clippings* as they are called, began, I daresay, with the advent of the first newspaper and it is

practised by nearly everybody, however otherwise sane
they may be. Some hobbyists save all of the political
articles; others, those of an economic nature; a few, those
that treat of religious things, many, those that make up
society gossip; a small percentage, those that have to do
with science; and the undertakers clip those that are
printed in the obituary column. To be of the slightest
value, however, the clippings must be properly filed and
there are two chief ways of doing this, to wit (1) put
them in envelops, and (2) paste them in scrapbooks.

If the clippings are of such a character that their alpha-
betic classification is necessary, then an envelop for each
different subject should be used. Suppose, for example,
you are collecting science clippings, you label the first
envelop *Astronomy*, the second one *Botany*, the third
Chemistry, and so on down to the last one which is *Zo-
ology*. But when you want to keep the articles in the sequence in which they appear as, for instance, the way that
actors and other people in the public eye do, then you
should paste them in a scrapbook.

About Collecting Newspapers.—It is said that there
is nothing so stale as yesterday's news. A taxi-driver,
with whom I used to ride in better days, has a somewhat
different idea of the old saw, and this he demonstrates by
his collection of old newspapers. For twenty years he has
saved those that carry headlines in 2-inch type across the
front page, like the sinking of the *Titanic*, and the *Lusi-
tania*, the San Francisco earthquake, our entry into the
World War, the signing of the Armistice, etc.

I looked over his collection the other day and it seemed
to me that the record he had of startling events consti-
tuted anything but stale news. Another thing that im-

pressed me was that he had the high spots of each event clearly in mind, and the way that he related them sounded as if each one was happening *now* and not yesterday. It was as good as a Burton Holmes' lecture and it seemed to me the taxi-driver had missed his calling—he should have been a professor of history instead of clocking a cab.

Collecting Pictures.—Many proletarians make collections of newspaper and magazine pictures, thousands of the middle class make collections of photographs, some of the intelligentsia make collections of etchings, while a few multi-millionaires make collections of the old masters.

I have seen collections of newspaper pictures that I would rather own than some of the collections of modern paintings, but regardless of personal taste whatever your idea of pictures is, and you are making a collection of, if you are doing it in the proper hobby spirit, that is you are getting the maximum pleasure out of it, this is all that matters.

The first thing to do is to make up your mind what kind of pictures you are going to collect and then let your conscience and pocketbook be your guide. The chief factor in making a collection of pictures, or anything else for that matter, is to know all that is knowable about each one, otherwise you might just as well buy a paper of pins and call it a collection for it will mean about as much to you.

Collecting Minerals and Semi-Precious Stones.— Making a collection of minerals and semi-precious stones will give you a hobby that is at once interesting and well worth while, especially if you like geology and chemistry. Now before we get into the matter of making a collection of them let's find out just what they are.

What we call a *mineral* is any kind of a chemical element or compound that is formed by natural processes from inorganic, that is, non-living, matter. All minerals are solid substances, except water and mercury at ordinary temperatures. Minerals and semi-precious stones have, in almost every case, a definite molecular structure and this gives them their characteristic form, and the optical properties of a crystal.

A *precious stone* is a mineral that is either quite scarce, or beautiful, or both, and, hence, it has a high commercial value. The true precious stones are limited to the diamond, ruby, emerald and sapphire.[12] A *semi-precious stone* is also a mineral, but as it is not at all scarce and has not the purity or beauty of a precious stone, it therefore has less commercial value.

How to Start a Mineral Collection.—There are several ways that you can start a mineral collection, and chief among these are (1) to go to the localities where they occur and find them, (2) to send to the different localities for them, and (3) to buy them of some dealer who specializes in them. The latter is, obviously, the easier and cheaper way.

The Washington School Collection.—You can get a collection consisting of 40 fair-sized specimens of minerals and rocks, each of which is labeled and all of them placed in a cloth-covered case with a separate tray for each one for $10.00 or less.[13]

The Twentieth-Century Collection.—This is a very good collection to start off with, as it includes not only

---

[12] The *pearl* is called a *precious stone*, but it is not a mineral as it is formed of organic matter.

[13] The Central Scientific Company, Chicago, Illinois, sells them.

40 different minerals and ores, but a sample of a finished product from each. The whole collection is placed in a cloth-covered box with a hinged cover and an index giving the name, chemical composition, chief source, product manufactured and chief uses. It will cost you in the neighborhood of *$20.00,* and it is shown in *Fig. 6.*

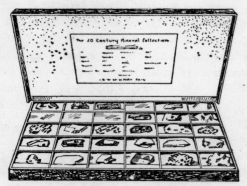

FIG. 6.—THE TWENTIETH-CENTURY MINERAL COLLECTION

The collection includes these minerals:

Apatite	Tincal	Pyrolusite
Cryolite	Malachite	Muscovite
Buxite	Tripolite	Fluorite
Stibnite	Emery	Feldspar
Asbestos	Gold Quartz	Cinnebar
Asphalt	Chalcophyrite	Silver in Rock
Barite	Siderite	Sulphur, native
Petroleum	Limonite	Cassiterite
Ozokorite	Gelana	Spalerite
Chromite	Magnesite	Calamine

A Radioactivity Mineral Collection.—There are quite a number of *radioactive minerals,* that is, minerals which give off spontaneously *alpha, beta* and *gamma* rays,[14]

[14] To learn about these rays read any textbook on college physics and college chemistry. *Kimball's College Physics,* published by Henry Holt

the waves or particles of which travel at high speed and act on a photographic plate and a fluorescent screen like X-rays. A study of these minerals will carry you far into the realms of physics and chemistry. By riding this hobby, pleasure will not only accrue to you, but you will gain a liberal education at the same time.

Partial List of Radioactive Minerals

Calc spar .... per piece $.75
Carnotite (radium ore) .... per piece $.25
Fluorspar cubes ($\frac{1}{2}$" square) .... per cube $.50
Kunzite, fluorescent .... per 7 grams $3.75
Thorium nitrate .... per oz. $.50
Uranium nitrate .... per oz. $.40
Uranium oxide (yellow) .... per oz. $.45
Willemite, fluorescent .... per oz. $.75
Willemite, phosphorescent .... per oz. $.75
Pitchblende .... per oz. $.50

A Semi-Precious Stone Collection.—This consists of 25 specimens, each in a tray and all in a hardwood case. It is listed at $10.00. Following is a list of the specimens:

Garnet	Beryl	Amazon stone	Chalcedony
Opal	Jasper	Green Feldspar	Porphyrite
Amethyst	Cat's-eye	Sapphire	Onyx
Carnelian	Agate	Lapis lazuli	Serpentine
Moonstone	Tourmaline	Bloodstone	
Zircon	Aquamarine	Quartz	
Topaz	Tiger's-eye	Rhodolite	

Other Mineral Collections.—You can either buy or build up several other kinds of mineral collections.

and Co., N. Y. and *Smith's Inorganic Chemistry,* published by D. Appleton-Century Co., N. Y., are good books for you to read.

Among these are specimens that (*1*) show a play of colors, a change of colors, opalescence, iridescence, tarnish, asterism, schillerization, fluorescence and phosphorescence; (*2*) illustrate the color, taste and feel; (*3*) serve for blowpipe analysis; (*4*) illustrate copper ores and minerals; (*5*) iron ores and minerals; (*6*) ores and minerals of gold, silver, platinum and iridium; (*7*) ores of various other metals; (*8*) non-metallic economic minerals, etc.

The Value of a Mineral Collection.—As in the collection of almost all other objects, the hobbyist who goes deeply into the study of minerals gets the most out of it, thereby fulfilling the platitude which states that you get out of life just what you put into it.

So the first thing to do is to get a textbook on *geology* and one on *college chemistry*. The geology will give you the history of the earth and its life as recorded in the rocks, and from the chemistry you will learn the composition of the various minerals and ores and the different crystalline forms they take. Knowing these things will put you on the road to a real education. Then add to this advantage the pleasure you will derive from the physical aspects of the various specimens of minerals in your collection.

Collecting and Preserving Insects.—The name *insect*, which is given to any of the numerous small invertebrate animals that has a body which is more or less segmented, comes from the Latin word *insectus* which means to *cut in*, and it is so called because the body seems to be cut in, or almost divided. Insects, or *Insecta* as this class is called, consist of two orders, namely, those that have (*1*) six legs and are winged, as the flies, bees, bugs, beetles, butterflies, etc., and (*2*) more than six legs and are wingless, as mites, ticks, wood lice, ants, spiders, centipedes, etc.

Now to be a collector of insects and enjoy it to the fullest as a hobby, you must be a born naturalist, by which I mean you must have an ingrowing desire to observe and study them and to know all about them. Of course, nearly every one knows the various insects by their common names when he sees them or feels them bite, but as to their interior and exterior construction and their classification, the average person knows very little or nothing.

Kinds of Insects.—There are roughly *22* orders of insects, and these are divided into from *1* to *80* or more families, these into from *1* to over *1,000* genera, and these, again, into from *1* to over *3,000* species. For your first collection it is a good scheme to make up one that has a single specimen of each of these divisions. Then after you have done this you can make a collection of any one of the families, genera, or species you may fancy.

The most brilliant, beautiful and showy of all the insects are, of course, the *butterflies,* which belong to the order of *Lepidoptera,*[15] and this includes about *50* families, over *700* genera, and *2,000* species. Wherever you live you will have no difficulty in collecting insects for they are plentiful everywhere. As an example, there are over *15,000* species of insects to be found within *50* miles of New York City, and of these there are more than *2,000* species of butterflies and moths.

[15] Pronounced Lep-i-*dop'*-ter-a.

How to Collect Insects.—If you want to make a collection of insects, then the first thing you must do is to learn how to gather and preserve them. If this is as far as your interest goes in *entomology*,[16] which is that branch of zoölogy that treats of insects, or *bugology* as the unlearned and vulgar call it, send to the secretary of *The American Museum of Natural History* for a copy

FIG. 7.—How to Preserve Insects

of the leaflet called *How to Collect and Preserve Insects,* which is, I believe, free. (See *Fig. 7.*)

If, however, you want to know what class, order, genera and species they belong to, their life histories—in a word, all about them, including the way to collect and preserve them, then get Dr. Frank E. Lutz's *Field Book of Insects.*[17] Dr. Lutz is the Curator of the Department of Entomology of the American Museum of Natural History, and he is one of the foremost authorities on *Insecta.*

[16] The word *entomology* comes from the Greek noun *entomos* which means *insect,* plus *logia* which means *science.*
[17] G. P. Putnam's Sons, New York. $2.50.

Collecting Birds' Eggs and Nests.—Birds' eggs and nests are certainly among the most interesting objects to be found in nature, and some of them are very beautiful and wonderful indeed. At some time in your young life you must have watched birds building their nests and admired the extraordinary skill and laborious efforts that they showed in making them.

About Collecting Birds' Nests.—Now a collection of nests built by various kinds of birds in your locality is easy to make and highly entertaining, and there is no real harm done in making one, since the birds seldom use the same nest twice, but other than the motive to provide a hobby there is nothing much to be gained by doing so since naturalists know everything that can be known about birds' nests.

Why Not to Collect Birds' Eggs.—There are a dozen reasons why you should *not* collect birds' eggs, or get, by purchase or otherwise, collections of them from others. Chief and most important among these reasons are (*1*) it is destructive to bird life, and (*2*) collecting eggs contributes nothing to the knowledge of them.

Of all the numerous other factors which destroy birds, collecting their eggs is the most wanton and disastrous, and this is particularly true of the larger and rarer birds because their eggs are, naturally, the most sought after by collectors. In England, several species of birds have been entirely exterminated because their eggs have been persistently taken by collectors, who are prevalent in that country.

There are numerous private collectors who have accumulated thousands of birds' eggs, without ever learning or publishing any scientific facts which could begin to compensate for this destruction of bird life. As a matter of fact, the egg shells, which are all that the egg collector preserves, are only of small importance, since, in the last analysis, they are all alike except in size and coloration, and all of the variations of both of these are already known. In nearly all cases the contents of the egg (that is, the developing embryo) which might be of some scientific value is blown out and into the sink by the egg-shell collector.

As most birds and their nests and eggs are protected by state and federal laws, and by the *International Treaty with Canada,* egg collecting can only be legally carried on by holders of permits from these authorities. Any one who has observed birds when they were laboriously building their nests and the patience with which they sit on the eggs day after day and night after night for two weeks, and much longer in the case of the larger birds, and often when they were in great danger to themselves, will surely realize that collecting birds' eggs is a very cruel and useless hobby and that it is nothing short of a crime to do so. *So don't do it!*

The Hobby of Collecting Dolls.—A doll is, as you well know, a puppet of a baby or a child that is made especially for little girls to play with. It is the maternal instinct in the female of the species that makes the doll so especially attractive to her, and very often this remains constant throughout her life, especially if she has had no babies of her own.

Now nearly every little girl has a nondescript collection of dolls, but to make a hobby that is worthy of a grown-up's intellect there must be a deeper motive back of it which is based on some kind of a system. Thus you can make a collection of (*1*) period dolls, and (*2*) of native dolls. Period dolls are those which represent the costumes worn by men and women of different historical times, while native dolls are those which represent men and women of the different races or countries.

To make a collection of period dolls, you must determine first what characters or personages you want them to represent, and then buy dolls whose heads seem to be the most appropriate for the purpose. You can paint the faces of the latter and make suitable wigs for them; this done, dress them up in historically correct costumes, and to do this to the best advantage you must study the dress of the times and the people who lived in them that you are going to imitate in doll form, and make them as nearly like the originals as you can.

To make a collection of native dolls you can proceed along two different lines. You can buy dolls and paint them, make wigs and dress them to look as nearly like the races or natives of the various countries as you can. If you live in a city, this is done easily enough, for you can consult the picture files of the art department that is connected with the public library and find exactly what you are looking for.

To make a collection of dolls that are of and by the natives themselves of various countries is something else again, for it is not at all an easy thing to do, but when you have finally accomplished it, it has a charm and interest that at once throws the imitation collection in the shade.

Now there are devious ways by which you can make such a collection and here are the chief ones: (*1*) pick them up when you are traveling in various countries,

(2) scout around among the different centralized nation-
alities in the big cities and find them, and (3) get in
touch with the American consuls in the large cities of
the different countries, and they will tell you where you
can buy them.

This latter method of getting native dolls is a slow and
a more or less costly one, but when you have completed
it you will have a collection which is at once authentic,
wonderful and of considerable intrinsic value. My good
friend, Ella B. Warner of the International House, *500*
Riverside Drive, New York City, makes a trip to Continental Europe every year in the interest of her gift
shop, and she usually has a number of dolls from different countries on hand, and if you will write to her, she
will give you some valuable pointers on making a collection of them.

Collecting Indian Curios.—For firing the imagination, there is no hobby that can begin to compete with
that of collecting Indian curios. Look at a chipped *arrowhead,* and you will see redskins lurking behind trees ready
to ambush the palefaces as they wend their way to the
meeting-house, or in their more peaceful pursuit of shooting down a herd of buffalo from the backs of their hard-
running ponies.

Pick up a *tomahawk* and instantly there looms up the
frightful image of *Lo* the poor Indian, burying the hatchet
—in the head of his white adversary. Examine the blood-
stained *knife* of a brave, and you will shudder as you
envision him holding the hair of a white victim in one
hand, while he deftly relieves him of his scalp with the
other; or breathlessly you watch him fight a hand-to-

hand battle with Buffalo Bill, or other famous frontiers-men.

Hold a *tom-tom* in your hands, and you will hear its rhythmic beat as the *Homo americanus* pounds it, the while making whoopee round the camp-fire before attacking a wagon train of the pioneers. Finally, gaze upon the *war-bonnet* of old *Chief Rain-in-the-Face,* or one of his contemporaries, and you will sense the shadowy presence of a proud and stately headsman of the Sioux, the Cheyennes, or the Apaches before you, as he directs the destinies of his tribe.

About the North American Indians.—Before we get into the details of collecting Indian curios let's take a look at the Indians themselves, and so get the *low-down* on the hobby. They can be divided into two general classes and these are (*1*) the primitive tribes who inhabited the territory that is now called the United States when Columbus discovered America, and for a goodly time thereafter, and (*2*) their descendants—the present-day tribes—who have been herded onto lands which are called *reservations* by our ever smiling Uncle Samuel.

The primitive tribes may be put into three groups, and these are (*a*) the Forest Tribes, (*b.*) the Plains Tribes, and (*c*) the Southwest Tribes. All of the *Forest Tribes* were agriculturists, fishermen and game hunters. They used *wampum* for money, chipped arrow-heads and axes from flint, and those of the *North Woods* made many things of birch-bark, including megaphones and canoes. All of these things were not only very useful but they were highly artistic as well.

The *Plains Tribes* are divided into two groups, the

Sedentary Tribes, as they are called, who lived from the products of the soil, and the *Nomadic Tribes,* who lived by the hunt. The former tribes built earth-covered huts which were often large enough to house *50* or more of them at a time.

The latter tribes got not only their food but almost all of the other necessities of life from the buffalo. The skins furnished them with clothing and covering for their wigwams or tents, while the horns were made into various implements of industry and war. They are particularly noted for their picture writing on leather and also for their quill, feather and beadwork. It is an interesting fact that the sedentary plains Indians made pottery, while the nomadic tribes confined their operations to light basketry which is easily transported.

The Indians of the Southwest were also divided into sedentary and nomadic tribes. The former lived in large *pueblos,* or community houses which they built either of stone blocks or *adobe* bricks, which latter were made of mud and baked in the sun to harden them. Their chief household utensils were made of pottery, and they were agriculturists. The early ancestors of these tribes were the *Cliff Dwellers,* and they also are known as the *Basket Makers* for they were expert in the art of basket weaving. These baskets they used for every conceivable purpose, even for burying their dead.

Some of the nomadic tribes of the Southwest lived on the more fertile areas of land and raised corn and beans, while other tribes had to obtain their food supplies almost wholly from the desert plants such as the cactus, yucca and mesquite. Another tribe, the *Navajos* (pronounced *Nav'*-a-hos), built log houses for their winter

homes and lived in brush shelters, using a cliff, or other
natural protection, for a wind-break for their summer
quarters.

They were an agricultural tribe and also raised large
herds of sheep. They are famous for their artistic blankets, which they wove from the wool of the sheep. Their
blanket weaving is believed to be of comparatively recent origin, that is to say since the invasion of the Spaniards. They are also expert silversmiths, and it is prob-
able that this art came down to them from the Mayas
or the Aztecs in the long ago.

How to Start an Indian Collection.—Indian curios are
of two general kinds: (*1*) the artifacts of the early Indians who lived in America when Columbus discovered
it for the benefit and behoof of the white race, and (*2*)
the artifices of the present-day Indians. You can make a
collection of the artifacts or the artifices, or both, as your
fancy dictates, and your time and funds will allow. The
artifacts consist chiefly of *wampum*,[18] which are beads
made of shells and used by Indians as money; arrow-
heads, axes and tomahawks of chipped flint, tobacco
pipes, and bowls for grinding corn. The *artifices* include
bows and arrows, baskets and pottery, blankets, beads and
feather work and silver ornaments of artistic design and
skilled workmanship.

Since the Indians inhabited every part of North America, you can find artifacts made by him wherever you
may live without any great amount of trouble. Thus you
might very naturally think that New York City, with
its teeming millions of inhabitants, would be about the

[18] So called from the Algonquin word *wamp* (from *wab* which means
white) plus *ompe* meaning a *string* (of shell beads).

last place where curios of the Indians could still be found; yet a few years ago some boys who were scratching around among the rocks in the vicinity of *207*th Street and Amsterdam Avenue,[19] found a number of

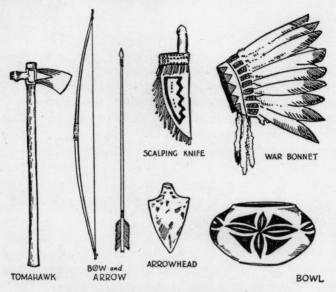

SCALPING KNIFE   WAR BONNET

TOMAHAWK   BOW *and* ARROW   ARROWHEAD   BOWL

Fig. 8.—A Collection of Indian Curios

arrow-heads and other artifacts, and later on they discovered the skeletons of two Indian women.

Some years ago when I lived in Rockland County, New York,[20] I picked up, at different times, on my tramps through the forests primeval, various artifacts (see *Fig. 8*), including a fine stone bowl. So almost anywhere you live, you can learn where the Indians had their

[19] This place is now a little park and is known as *Rock Shelter*.
[20] This is only *28* miles from New York City.

villages or camped, and there you will be apt to find objects of their handiwork. Nearly every city has its curiosity shop and among its varied oddments are always to be found a few Indian curios for sale.

For primitive and modern Indian goods, you can buy all you want of them if you pay a visit to some reservation. If this is not possible you can write to the *United States Indian Agents* at the various reservations,[21] and they will tell you who sells them. Then there are numerous dealers scattered throughout the country who handle Indian goods and you can get the names and addresses of these from a paper called the *North American Indian Relic Collectors Bulletin,* which is published at *5022* North Lockwood Avenue, Chicago, Illinois. A couple of them that I can give you off-hand are Miss Grace Nickelson, *46* Los Robles Street, Pasadena, California, and J. E. Standley, Old Curiosity Shop, Seattle, Washington.

If you live or are sojourning in New York City, be sure to go and see the very fine collection of artifacts and artifices at the *Museum of the North American Indian* which is located at *155*th Street and Broadway. There is no admission charge and it is open from *2* to *5* every afternoon. For any expert advice on Indian curios, write the Curator of the museum, who will gladly give it to you without cost.

[21] You can get the names of these from the Secretary of the Department of the Interior, Washington, D. C.

CHAPTER III

SOME PLANT HOBBIES

THE first hobby that man ever rode was the caring and raising of plants, or *horticulture,* as it is now called; and on down through the ages it has appealed more and more to him until today it is the most universal and best beloved of all the natural and artificial devices that are his to choose from for refreshing his spirit and sustaining his body.

There is something about the planting of a seed, a bulb, a slip, or seedling, then tending it carefully and watching it grow, that makes an infinite appeal to the human mind, and this regardless of age, sex or mentality; hence it follows, it goes a long way toward inspiring the hobbyist to nobler thoughts and gentler actions, and so making the world a better place to live in.

Now besides the afflatus and gratification that you will get out of initiating plants and watching them grow, is the sensual delight you will derive from their symmetry, their beauty, and ofttimes, their exquisite odor, as, for example, the rose, which is a perfect blend of all these factors. Besides these marvels, others will be unfolded to you if you will but dig deeper into the nature of plants, when you will get about as close to the origin of life as it is humanly possible to get at the present time.

To do this you must make a study of *botany,* as the

general science of plants is called, and after you have gained a fairly good idea of the fundamentals of it you can then take up the various specialized branches, each one of which is a deep and abiding hobby in its own right, and all of which I shall tell you a little about as we push along. And now let's go back to the beginning and start off the various horticultural hobbies with the simple growing of plants.

The Hobby of Growing Plants.—To make the growing of plants a hobby, you can have (*1*) a few pots of them indoors, or (*2*) a whole garden of them outdoors. Further, you can grow (*a*) food plants, (*b*) tropical plants, (*c*) flowering plants, or (*d*) fruit plants.

By *food plants* are meant those of a succulent nature, i. e., having watery tissues, and these include practically all of the vegetables that are good to eat. The *tropical plants,* as their name infers, are those that had their origin in tropical or semi-tropical countries, and these include the *cacti,*[1] which are likewise succulent plants, though their outward appearance does not at all indicate it. The *flowering plants* are those that produce conspicuous flowers and seeds, and, finally, *fruit plants* are those that produce flowers, fruit and seeds. So you see there are many varieties of plants for you to choose from.

The Hobby of Indoor Plant Culture.—By *indoor plants* are meant any and all of those that you can grow in a living-room or a school-room the year round. To grow them successfully you must see that (*1*) a good potting soil is used,[2] (*2*) they are watered properly, (*3*) a tem-

---

[1] This is the Latin plural for *cactus,* and it is used in horticultural parlance in preference to the English plural *cactuses.*

[2] A good potting soil can be had by mixing 2 parts of garden soil, *1* part of leaf mold and *1* part of sand.

perature of 65 to 70 degrees is maintained during the day, and that it does not fall more than 10 degrees during the night and, lastly, (4) that they have enough light.

Plants for the Living- and School-room.—There are, as you know, a large number of plants that can be grown indoors, and these can be raised from seed, slips, bulbs and seedlings. Some of them, including all of those of the bulb kind, must have (1) plenty of sunlight, while others can get along with (2) very little light.

Plants That Need Sunlight.—If you can have a window-box in a south or a southwest window, or if you can keep your plants in some other place where there is a lot of sunshine, the following kinds of plants will thrive admirably: [3] (a) the *Azalea indica,* (b) ever-blooming begonia (*Begonia semperflorens*), (c) scarlet begonia (*Begonia coccinea*), (d) coral begonia (*Begonia maculata*), (e) colens (various garden varieties), (f) common, fancy and Lady Washington geraniums (*Pelargonium domesticum*), (g) zonal geranium (*Pelargonium zonal*), (h) halsam (*Impatiens sultani*), (i) flowering maple (*Abutilion*), (j) the primrose (*Primula*), and (k) the bulbs.

Among the bulbs that you can grow in pots with soil are (a) the grape hyacinth, (b) white calla lily, (c) freesia calla lily and the giant snowdrop; those that you can grow in fiber, i. e., in prepared root, are (a) lily of the valley, and (b) the Roman hyacinth; in fiber and water, the white paper narcissus, and, in water alone, the hyacinth.

[3] The following list of plants was compiled by Ellen Eddy Shaw, Curator of Elementary Education, at the Brooklyn Botanic Garden, Brooklyn, N. Y.

Plants That Need Little Light.—If your plants can get but little light then you must limit them largely to those known as *foliage plants,* so called because they are noted for the beauty of their foliage. The chief ones are (*a*) the asparagus ferns [4] (*A. pulmosus* and *A. sprengeri*), (*b*) common aspidistra (*Aspidistra lyrida*), (*c*) rex begonia (*Begonia rex*), (*d*) silver-spotted begonia (*Begonia argenteo-grittata*), (*e*) fountain plant (*Cordyline indivisa*), (*f*) Croton (*Croton variegatum*), (*g*) dragon plant (*Dracœna fragrans*), (*h*) ferns, Boston and Christmas, (*Pteris,* Maidenhair), (*i*) pandamus (*Pandamus veitchii*), (*j*) peperomia (*Peperomia saundersii*), (*k*) snake plant (*Sanservieria*), and, lastly, (*l*) the strawberry geranium (*Saxifraga sarmentosa*).

Should you use a window-box for your plants it is a good scheme to put a *trailer* in front of it, and this can be (*a*) the wandering Jew (*Tradescantia*), (*b*) English ivy, (*c*) trailing or drooping colens, (*d*) Saxifraga sarmentosa, (*e*) geranium ivy, (*f*) climbing fig (*Ficus pumila*), and (*g*) the *Zebrina pendula.*

Plants in Apartments.—Steam-heated apartments are not very well suited for keeping ordinary plants because the atmosphere is usually too warm and too dry. This condition, however, is where the *cacti* shine for they will thrive where the softer plants will die. This does not mean that they do not need looking after, but their three chief needs are (*1*) air, (*2*) sunlight and (*3*) sharp drainage.

To secure the latter they should be planted in bowls

[4] The ferns belong to the order *Filicales* and to the phylum *Pteridophyta.* They resemble seed plants in having three parts, i. e., root, stem and leaves, or *fronds* as they are called, and in having vascular tissues.

or pots that have a thick layer of stones on the bottom,
or broken pieces of pots will do, with the spaces filled in
with charcoal; then a layer of sandy soil on top of this
but which has no manure or other fertilizer in it. Some
varieties such as the Christmas cacti (*Epiphyllum trunœ-
tum*), and the night-blooming cereus (*Cereus grandi-
florus*) need a heavier soil but without any fertilizer. A
good book for you to read is *The Cactus Book* by
A. D. Houghton.[5]

For further information *re* plants, their care and prop-

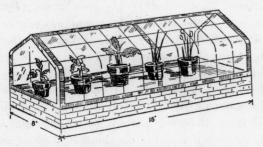

FIG. 9.—THE KIDDIES' GREENHOUSE

agation for the living- and school-room write to the
School Nature League, American Museum of Natural
History, New York City, for copies of the *Bulletins* it
issues. The various *State Colleges of Agriculture,* and
the *United States Department of Agriculture,* Washington, D. C., also issue bulletins and pamphlets on the indoor and outdoor culture of plants of all kinds.

About Greenhouse Plant Culture.—*The Kiddies'
Greenhouse.*—This little greenhouse, which is shown in
Fig. 9, is a cute replica of its big brothers, and when it
is stocked with plants, it makes a hobby the kiddies will

[5] The Macmillan Co., New York City, *$2.50.*

love and so get them started on the way to other and
more pretentious plant hobbies. It has a steel frame and
is enclosed with a celluloid composition so that there is no
glass to break. It comes in three different sizes, the smallest of which costs $2.95, the medium, $5.95, and the largest, $7.50.[6]

Little folks can plant and cultivate their own seeds,
and so get the thrill of tending and watching the shoots
develop into healthy plants. While, of course, flowering
plants are the most interesting in the long run, some of
the succulent plants, such as radishes, lettuce, etc., come
up the quickest and will, therefore, be of greater interest
to the little minds. You can get seeds, slips and small
plants at a very small cost from nurseries, department
stores and at the 5 and 10 cent stores.

The Hobby of Outdoor Plant Culture.—Is it your
earnest desire to live to a ripe old age—say a hundred
years, or thereabouts? If so, well, here's how to do it. The
formula you have to follow is a very simple one, for all
you have to do is *to make and tend a garden*—of whatever size and kind it doesn't much matter. In all fairness
I must admit I have only two-thirds proved my theory by
personal experience, but I am firm in my belief that it is
right, for I am still going strong. Now there are several
kinds of gardens, and chief among these are (1) the
vegetable garden, (2) the flower garden, (3) the rock
garden, and (4) the water garden.

About Your Vegetable Garden.—Planting and raising vegetables will not only serve to ease your wearied
brain, but if you are a convalescent, or are anæmic, or

[6] These little greenhouses are made by The Meccano Company of
America, Inc., 200 Fifth Avenue, New York City.

getting along in years, and with nothing else to do in particular, close contact with the soil, the plants that grow in it and the ultra-violet rays of the sun will all help mightily to mend you and keep you fit to carry on, for they are Nature's greatest healing agents. (See *Fig. 10.*)

Then, what's more, Scotch as it may seem, you eat the things you have so lovingly raised, and when you do this

FIG. 10.—HOW TO LIVE TO BE 100 YEARS OLD

you will, of a certes, know that they are fresh; this being true, it follows that all of the health- and life-giving vitamins which they contain will be transfused into you and so make you well and strong and happy again, in which case the *Grim Reaper* will be staved off a little while longer.

Now it is not my intention here to tell you how to make a vegetable garden and what to raise in it, for I take it you know as much about it as I do, or the next one. To find out all about the various kinds of vegetables you

want to raise, send to the different dealers in seeds, bulbs
and seedlings for their catalogues—and gorgeous ones
they are too.[7]

You will find their advertisements in nearly every paper and magazine that is published. There are, also,
numerous books that tell you everything you may want
to know about all kinds of gardening.[8]

About Your Flower Garden.—Of all the beautiful
things on earth the most beautiful are beautiful flowers.[9]
The lowly man is rich indeed who has a flower garden;
the richest man who lives in a duplex apartment or a
swell hotel and hasn't one is a pauper. The most hardened
criminal in prison prizes the privilege of having one, and
the sanctimonious cuss who doesn't care for one is likely
to find the gates of heaven locked against him and the
key thrown away.

The love of flowers, the outward expression of which
is to own and care for a flower garden (see *Fig. 11*), is the
only true religion and he who tends it can't stray very
far from the straight and narrow path. Go then, thou
infidel, and make yourself a flower garden and you will
be cleansed of your iniquities even as a dip into the
Ganges washes away the sins of the Hindu.

Now, just as there are multitudinous kinds of flowers,
so, also, are there almost as many kinds of flower gardens. But the thing is to have one, whether it is a little
square or circular spot in the front or back yard, or an

[7] Write to Peter Henderson and Company, 35 Cortlandt Street, and to
Stumpp and Walter Company, 132 Church Street, both of New York City,
for their catalogues.

[8] You can get the names and prices of them from the Orange Judd
Publishing Company, 15 East 26th Street, New York City.

[9] My apologies to Gertrude Stein. (She's got me doing it now.)

elaborately laid-out plot artistically landscaped for the purpose. Since, as in all other things, tastes materially differ in the matter of flowers, it follows that some folks love those grown in the old-fashioned gardens, while others dote upon the more recent, highly cultured kind.

The three things about flowers that makes the strongest appeal to the senses of mankind are their brilliant colors, marvelous forms, and exquisite odors. Some kinds

FIG. 11.—A FLOWER GARDEN

of flowers have all of these qualities, as for instance the rose and the Easter lily; others have beautiful colors and forms but no odor, and still others may have only a pleasing odor to recommend them, as the mignonette.

Should you have only a small space for your flower bed, you may prefer an assortment of flowers, so that you will have an intermingled collection of colors and forms. If you can have several beds, then massed flowers of a single, or an allied kind, will make the most striking showing. Your individual taste, and this is largely governed by your artistic temperament, must determine the

kinds of flowers you will grow in your garden as well as
the arrangement of them.

I shall not attempt to give you the names of the flowers
for your garden for there is an enormously long list of
them and these you can raise from seed, bulbs, roots
and seedlings. The popular flowers grown from seed alone
number *300* kinds or more, and these can be divided into
some *15* groups for various uses. To find out the kind you
want, all about them, and when and how to plant them,
send to the various large dealers for their catalogues and
you will find all of them or, at least, the most popular
ones, printed in their natural colors and described in
picturesque detail.

Then there are many very good books on floriculture,
and if you are a novice at the hobby you should by all
means read one or more of them before you make your
garden. You can get these books at any public library,
or buy them of dealers in things for the garden.

About Your Rock Garden.—Properly, a *rock garden*
is one that is laid out in a rocky place and which is particularly adapted for alpine and dwarf plants. You can,
however, make an *artificial rock garden* in your yard or
other plot of ground, and there are numerous kinds of
plants that will thrive in it, the chief ones of which I
shall tell you about a little farther along.

How to Make It. [10]—Your rock garden can be located
any place you may have room for it, but if a bank or a
mound is already there, you can make it with far less

[10] Write Peter Henderson and Company, *35* Cortlandt Street, New
York, for their pamphlet, *How to Build a Rock Garden,* and it will be
sent free to you, and also a list of hardy rock garden plants. You can
get further information from the American Rock Garden Society, *552*
Fifth Avenue, New York City.

effort. If the ground is more or less level, then you will have to build up a base of ordinary soil. This done, set the stones on it so that it will look as if the hand of nature had done the job instead of your own delicate ones.

Set some of the stones into the ground quite deep, then lay the others on the surface and, finally, roll a couple of large ones into appropriate positions. You must leave enough space between the stones for the plants to grow, and to make them grow well, put a layer of rich soil on top of the ordinary soil. To prevent air spaces between them you must work the soil well around the stones.

If you use perennial flower seed you must put them in a year ahead of the time they are to bloom, and plant them early in the spring and on up to the middle of July. To have flowers in the spring you can plant tulip and other bulbs in your rock garden, or you can put in hardy plants. There are a couple of dozen of these and by carefully choosing them, you can have flowers that bloom every month from April until October.

About Your Water Garden.—Water and water life have an irresistible charm for the kiddies, and a *water garden* with some water plants and gold or other kinds of fish in it will entertain them for hours on end. Contrary to what your preconceived ideas on the subject may be, you can easily make a water garden at a very small cost.

How to Make It.—There are several ways that you can make the pool, the simplest of which is to sink a washtub in the ground until the edge of the former is flush with the surface of the latter, and be sure to have it in a sunny place. This done half-fill the tub with rich soil, then cover this with a layer of white sand and fill it to the brim with water.

Put a water milfoil, a water poppy, or some other kind of a submerged plant in it to supply oxygen to the water, and also a water lily to give an aquatic look to the surface of the pool; then stock it with a few fish and, finally, put some water-absorbing plants along the outside edge of the tub when your water garden is done, and it will not need any further attention on your part.

By spending a little more money you can build a pool 5 or 6 feet in diameter of stone and concrete, and to do this dig a hole with an irregular outline about 18 inches deep and of the size you want it to be. Now pick up enough flat stones to cover the bottom and sides of the hole, and lay these as closely together as you can. Use the roughest stones for the sides, and fill in the spaces with smaller stones.

The final operation is to fill in the cracks with cement, and be sure you don't miss any of them. When it is done, it will make a rough, natural-looking, water-tight pool. Now put a layer of soil on the bottom and one of sand on this, put in some aquatic plants and a few fancy fish. According to my friend, William B. Lamb, who built one, the total cost for the necessary materials will be about 60 cents, or at least that is what it cost him.

To make an all cement pool will cost you considerably more, and it must be built in a certain way to keep it from shrinking and cracking; to do this takes several weeks and then it must be filled with water and emptied several times until all of the alkali in the concrete is removed. Alkali in the water would kill the fish. A concrete pool should have a drain pipe and a feeder pipe which is connected with a water supply pipe.

Before you make a water garden you should read *Small*

Pool Construction (*10* cents), and *Making Lily Pools* (*20* cents).[11] Should you want to build a larger pool get *Garden Pools Large and Small,* by Leonidas W. Ramsey and Charles H. Lawrence.[12]

Scientific Plant Hobbies.—As I have already explained, *botany* is the general science of plants, and the various specialized branches of it are (*a*) *genetics,* which deals with heredity and the variation of species; (*b*) *cytology,* which treats of the individual cells the plants are formed of; (*c*) *morphology,* of their external forms; (*d*) *histology,*[13] their internal structure; (*e*) *physiology,* of their life processes; (*f*) *ecology,* the mutual relationship between plants and their environment; (*g*) *taxonomy,* of their classification; (*h*) *phytogeography,* of their distribution, and (*i*) *pathology,* of their diseases.[14]

About the Breeding of Plants.—The word *breeding* means the begetting, or the procreating of living things with particular reference to improving breeds or strains of them, and so bringing out their best points; and the *breeding of plants* means that various varieties are improved by crossing them in accordance with what is known as *Mendel's law,* and on this is based the branch science of *genetics.*

I have not the space here to go into the details of breeding plants but I can give you a very good idea of

[11] Both of these are published by *The American Home,* Garden City, L. I., New York.

[12] Published by the Macmillan Company, N. Y., *$2.50.*

[13] This is called the *anatomy* of plants.

[14] All of these subjects, except pathology, are treated in the *University Text Book of Botany,* by Douglas Houghton Campbell, and published by the Macmillan Co., New York City. A good book on pathology is the *Manual of Plant Diseases,* by Frederick de Forest Heald, published by the McGraw-Hill Pub. Co., New York City.

how it is done by telling you a little about the experiments made by Gregor J. Mendel [15] in crossing peas, and from the results of which he formulated his famous law. Briefly, this law shows that the height, color and all other characteristics of plants depend on the presence of certain governing units in the germ cells of the seed, and in any given one of these the units are either present or absent.

Mendel took two pea plants one of which was very tall, about *6* feet high, and the other very short (dwarf) about *1* foot high, and crossed them, which is an easy thing to do. His first step was to pick the unbroken pair of anthers [16] out of the flower of the tall plant and to put on the stigma [17] of this the pollen [18] of the flower of the short plant. Now when the cross-bred seed which were produced by these two oppositely disposed plants grew up he found that all of them were tall.

When the seeds of these latter plants, which were produced by self-fertilization, grew up, some of them were tall and others were short like their grandparents. When the seeds of the tall plants and those of the short plants were planted by themselves, it was found that all of the former grew tall, i. e., they were *pure* in the strain of tallness, while all of the latter grew short, i. e., they were pure in the strain of shortness.

These governing units of heredity in the germ-cells also produce variously-colored flowers, double flowers,

[15] He was an Austrian Augustinian abbot who lived from 1822 to 1884.

[16] The *anther* is that part of the stamen in seed plants which develops and contains pollen.

[17] The *stigma* is that part of the pistil of a flower which receives the pollen grains and on which they germinate.

[18] The *pollen* is the mass of microspores in seed plants.

orchid-flowered varieties and other characteristics, in plants. To learn how to produce new varieties and strains, and hybrid flowers and units read *Fundamentals of Plant Breeding* by John M. Coulter, Ph.D., head of the Department of Botany, University of Chicago.[19]

[19] Published by D. Appleton-Century Company, N. Y.

CHAPTER IV

SOME ANIMAL HOBBIES

PART I

FOUR-FOOTED ANIMALS

To have a dog, a cat, a bird or any other animal that is higher or lower than these in the scale of nature is, simply, to have a pet. This being true, when then do animals serve the noble purpose of constituting a hobby? Well, the answer is, in several ways, and chief among these are when you (*1*) breed them, (*2*) show them for points, and (*3*) make an intensive study of them.

To *breed them* means that you mate them so that they will reproduce their kind; to *show them for points* means that you exhibit them in competition with others of the same breed at shows which are given by clubs and societies for the purpose of getting a blue ribbon, or perhaps a red one will do, and the perquisites that go with it in the shape of a cup or other prize; and, perchance to *sell them*, in which case the hobby just naturally dissolves in the acid of commercialism and the residue becomes a business.

What an Animal Is.—Now before we get into the subject of making animals serve the purposeful job of providing hobbies, let's find out just what an animal is. As you quite likely know, the name *animal* includes all kinds of living creatures that are endowed with the attributes of sensation and voluntary motion; and it follows, then, that a bacterium is as much of an animal as is a man, and the other way about.

About the Breeding of Animals.—The breeding of animals follows the same hereditary law as the breeding of plants, i. e., the *Mendelian law* which I told you about in the preceding chapter, and the purpose of it is the same, to wit, improving the breed, or the strain, so as to bring out its best points. There are different kinds of breeding but the two chief ones are (*1*) inbreeding and (*2*) cross-breeding.

By *inbreeding* is meant breeding from a male and a female of the same parentage, or from mates that are very closely related to each other. To get offspring of as pure a strain as possible, inbreeding is resorted to. This is the method that is used in Northern Africa and Southwestern Asia to produce the perfect breeds of horses and camels that are found there. The purer the strain of the animal the more delicate is apt to be its health and the harder it is to raise it. To get a pure breed of any kind of an animal and at the same time have it healthy and strong is not altogether an easy thing to do.

What is called a *thoroughbred* is an animal that is produced by *cross-breeding*. Thus the English thoroughbred race-horses have come down from a breed of recorded ancestry that is so old its origin is not with certainty known. It is believed to be the result of cross-breeding the barb, i. e., the Barbary horse,[1] and Arabian and Turkish blooded horses. The American thoroughbred, of which the great *Man-o'-War* was an example, comes from the

[1] One of a breed of horses related to the *Arabian* which is noted for its speed and endurance and which was introduced into Spain by the Moors.

English thoroughbred, and is practically identical with it.

If you are interested in breeding animals of any kind read up on heredity, Mendel's law, breeding and hybridization; you will find articles on these allied subjects in the various encyclopedias and in numerous books that have been published about them. You can get these in any good library. A very good book for you to own is *The Basis of Breeding* by Leon F. Whitney.[2]

About Animal Shows.—Dog, cat, bird and other animal shows are given all over the country and are both local and national in scope. If you have a pure-bred dog and want to enter it in a show, you should subscribe for the *American Kennel Gazette,* published at *221* Fourth Avenue, New York City, and become a member of the *American Kennel Club, Inc.,* of the same address.

The *Gazette* will give you a list of all the important dog shows throughout the country. You will also find in it a wealth of information concerning pure-bred dogs and the breeding of them. There is also a good little paper called *The Dog World,* published by the *Judy Publishing Company, 3,323* Michigan Boulevard, Chicago, Illinois.

Should you have a pure-bred cat that you want to enter, get the *Cat World Magazine,* published at *2,541* North Central Avenue, Chicago, Illinois, or *The Cat Courier,* published at *1,720* Randolph Street, Detroit, Michigan. Either of these papers will give you a list of the cat shows that are to be held. You should also join a cat club and you can find out the one that is the nearest to you by writing to the Secretary of *The United Cat Clubs of America,* Greenwich, Connecticut.

[2] Published by E. C. Fowler, 108 State St., New Haven, Conn.

The Dog Fancier Hobby.—*How to Start a Kennel.*
—Should it be your earnest desire to start a kennel as a
hobby, you can do so by either (*1*) buying a pure-bred
bitch of the breed you want and then mating her with
a properly selected pedigreed stud which is owned by
some fancier who keeps it at service, or (*2*) acquire both
a bitch and a stud and mate them at your own kennel.

FIG. 12.—A DOG THAT PLAYED A LEADING STAGE RÔLE

Jetta Fortunate Fields guided her master, William Williams, in
Windows, a play showing the value of the dog guide to the blind,
which was presented by the Seeing Eye Foundation.

You will find numerous advertisements in the dog papers
of owners who have studs at service, and bitches and
studs for sale. A pure-bred dog is pictured in *Fig. 12.*

In breeding dogs it is not advisable to keep too large
a litter or the puppies are apt to be undernourished and,
it follows, undersized. They must have plenty of room,
light and air and given the very best of care, for all of
these things are necessary to insure them having good

health. When they are weaned you must see to it that they are fed properly, for no matter how pure-blooded they are if they are not carefully reared they will not stand a ghost of a chance of ever being prize winners.

To learn all about the various breeds of dogs, their points and how they are judged, you should read *Pure-Bred Dogs,* the official book compiled by the Committee of the American Kennel Club.[3] It gives you the standards of some *150* breeds which are recognized by the American Kennel Club, Inc.

How Dogs Are Judged.—Since there are many different breeds of dogs it is obvious that each one must be judged by different standards. The standards for each breed are drawn by its own Specialty Club, that is, the club which fosters its individual interest. These standards are then submitted to the Committee of the American Kennel Club, and when they are passed upon and allowed by it, the judge of the Dog Show uses them when he is making his decisions for that particular breed.

Just to give you an idea of the standards that a given breed is judged by, let's take the Boston terrier as an example, as this is the most registered dog at the present time. This dog is bred for its smartness, intelligence and remarkable qualities of companionship. It is impatient and impetuous, characteristics which are due to its willingness to please and serve. It is always on the alert and makes an ideal house dog.

The Boston terrier is a recently established breed with a smooth coat, and it is really more of a bulldog than a terrier. It usually has a brindle color, with a smooth face,

[3] Published by G. Howard Watt, New York, *$5.00.*

widely separated eyes, straighter legs than a bulldog,
and it weighs from *15* to *30* pounds. A dog of this breed
is disqualified if it has (*1*) either a black, black and tan,
a liver, or a mouse color, (*2*) a Dudley-nose, (*3*) a
docked tail, or (*4*) any artificial means is used to deceive the judge. The points by which each breed are
judged always total *100*. The ring manners of a dog, i. e.,
his behavior while he is being judged, is always taken
into consideration though it does not figure in the listed
points.

Standards for Boston Terriers

General appearance	10	Forelegs	5
Skull	12	Hindlegs	5
Eyes	5	Feet	5
Muzzle	12	Tail	5
Ears	2	Color	4
Neck	3	Ideal Markings	10
Body	15	Coat	3
Elbows	4	TOTAL POINTS	100

The Cat Fancier Hobby.—*How to Start a Cattery.*—
What I have said above about starting a kennel holds
equally as good for starting a cattery, to wit, you can
buy a pure-bred female of whatever breed you are interested in, and mate her with a pedigreed stud that is
owned by some fancier, or you can buy a male and a female and mate them at your own cattery. You will find
both pedigreed males and females advertised in the cat
papers, I have previously cited. The care of kittens follows about the same procedure as for those of puppies.
Before you take up cats as a hobby I would, however,
suggest that you read C. H. Lane's book called *Rabbits,*

Cats and Cavies,[4] as this will give you a detailed description of the various breeds. *Fig. 13* shows *Silver Dick*, a pedigreed cat.

How Cats Are Judged.—Cats are judged by the general conformation and balance of their bodies, and they must show no trace of ranginess. Their heads must be big, full and round, and the eyes big, round and have a pleasant look. The color of them must conform to a certain stand-

Fig. 13.—Silver Dick, Owned by P. L. Evans, East St. Louis, Illinois

ard, i. e., they must be blue for a white cat, emerald green for a light silver, or chinchilla,[5] as this breed is called, and a deep yellow, or orange, for all other kinds.

Short-haired cats should have hair of a smooth and soft texture, while long-haired cats should have hair that is fine, silk-like and glossy. An important feature in all long-haired cats is the frill, or *Lord Mayor's Chain,* as it is

[4] This is published by the J. M. Dent Company, London, and you should be able to get it at your public library.

[5] So called because their color is very like that of a chinchilla, which is a pearly gray.

called, which is the tufted hair around its neck where the fur of the latter points up and that of the cheeks point down.

White-haired cats should have pure white hair; blue or slate ones should have no light shadings or undercolors; smoked ones should have a deep plum color with silver underneath; orange ones should be deep and rich, while tortoise-shell ones, which are the black and yellow mottled kind, should have the patches of these colors sharply defined.

The Rabbit Fancier Hobby.—*How to Start a Rabbitry.*—While pure-bred dogs and cats are rather costly hobbies and, hence, may be out of your financial reach, you can certainly indulge your animal-loving desires in a rabbitry. A pair of pure-bred rabbits of any of the various breeds can be had from *$5.00* to *$25.00,* and having these and a properly made hutch or hutches, your troubles will be over as far as your initial outlay of capital is concerned.

The ability of the doe to produce rapidly and in great numbers is truly amazing, since it breeds *7* times a year, and brings forth *7* or *8* young ones at a time. Assuming that this should take place without a break for *4* years or so, the young of a single pair will reach the startling figure of more than a million.

Rabbits are excellent animals to make experiments with the Mendelian law, as the following goes to show. A fancier in England some years ago found a rabbit in his breed that had only one ear. He watched the young of it and his ardent hopes were fulfilled: he found one of the opposite sex that likewise had only one ear. He mated these two

rabbits with the result that a breed of one-eared rabbits
were produced.

There are over a dozen different breeds of rabbits, and
of these the *Angora* [6] is the most beautiful. The price you
pay for its beauty is not in yens or kopecks, but in eternal
vigilance in caring for it. It has long, white, fleecy hair
that is as soft as silk, and to keep it from mating and in
good show form will take up about all of your spare waking
hours.

Another favorite fancy breed is the *Lop,* as the lop-
eared rabbit is called, and this is the *King* of the rabbit
tribe. It has very long and broad pendulous ears, which
measure some *6* inches across and about *26* inches in
length. You will find a complete description of all of the
various breeds of rabbits in C. H. Lane's book on *Rabbits,
Cats and Cavies.* When you get ready to buy rabbits,
write to the editor of *Wiedman's Rabbit Farmer, 1,615*
Redfield Street, La Crosse, Wisconsin, for a free copy.
In it you will find a number of fanciers listed who breed
and sell rabbits.

How Rabbits Are Judged.—Like all other animals, different breeds of rabbits have points all their own, and so
it is hard to formulate a set of fixed rules for all of them.
Generally speaking, however, the body of the rabbit should
be lower at the shoulders and should curve gracefully up-
wards to nearly the hind quarters.

It (the body) should be full and firm but still it must not
bulge with fat. The fore and hindlegs should be straight,
eyes a little convex rather than concave, and they should

---

[6] Angora is a city in Asia Minor, and it is supposed that the Angora
cat, rabbit and goat originally came from this part of the country.

have an agile appearance and a healthy look. With Lop rabbits, the breadth of the ears and the length of them are important factors, for the longer and wider they are the more points they count.

The Guinea-Pig Hobby.—*How to Start a Caviary.*— The guinea-pig, as the *cavy* is commonly called, did not come from *Guinea,* nor is it related to the pig, so whence cometh the name? Originally it was called the *pig cavy* because of its comparatively large body and little legs like a pig, and cavy from Cavia which is its generic name. Later on it was called a *cavy-pig* and this was corrupted to *guinea-pig.*

The cavy, or guinea-pig, is a little animal about *6* inches long, and it has a rounded nose, short ears that point toward the front part of its head, conspicuous eyes, *4* toes on each of its forefeet and *3* toes on each of its hindfeet. It can live, apparently, without water, its supply being had from that which is in its food, but it is a good scheme to have a little pure water always within its reach.

It is an adorable bit of livestock and makes the finest kind of an animal hobby, since it is perfectly harmless, as it does not bite or scratch, and it is clean, soft and pretty. It soon gets used to being handled and if you ever become interested in breeding them it's a *98* per cent bet that you will be an enthusiastic fancier to the end of your born days.

There are several varieties of cavies, the common ones being pure white, all black, red, cream, chocolate, blue, brindle and tortoise shell. The chief fancy cavies are the *Agenti* [7] which are silver-gray and golden-gray. The *Peru-*

[7] This is the native name of a breed that comes from South and Central America and the West Indies.

vians [8] are unique in that they are covered from muzzle
to breech with long, silky hair. When you have solved the
mystery of which end is which, you will find that they offer
the widest scope for breeding for show purposes. Other
fancy breeds are the Abyssinian, the Himalayan and the
Dutch, and you will find a description of all of them in
Lane's book, *Rabbits, Cats and Cavies.*

You can start a caviary with a single pair of cavies
or, better, if you can afford it, with a pair of each of the
different breeds. There are several fanciers in the United
States who have pure-bred cavies for sale and among these
are the *Scottdale Caviary,* Scottdale, Pennsylvania,
Mrs. Lawrence Lewis, 310 Lake Avenue, Govans, Baltimore, Maryland, and *Edwin L. Deicke,* of Lombard, Illinois. Mr. Deicke has written a book called *Cavies for
Pleasure and Profit* which contains a mine of information
as it tells all about the different breeds of cavies, gives
you the correct breeding methods, explains how to build
hutches, how to feed them, doctor them when sick and,
finally, show them off to the best advantage.

How Cavies Are Judged.—As an example of the way
that cavies are judged for points, take the Peruvian breed.
Its head should be rather long with a broad and rounded
muzzle and a Roman-shaped nose; the head and face
should be almost covered with hair falling over them like
that of a Skye terrier.

Its eyes should be large, full and bright, and except in
a pure white specimen, they should be of a dark color. Its
body should be broad and long as this gives it a better
carriage and adds points to its appearance. Finally, its hair

[8] You can get Peruvian cavies from L. W. Herold, Dumbarton, Maryland, or A. V. Suffers, *2,996* Garland Avenue, Detroit, Michigan.

should be soft and silky and the more of it that covers the
body and the longer it is, the more points it will score.

The White Rat Hobby.—*How to Start a Rattery.*—
Breeding rats as a hobby does not listen so good, but
just as there are men and men, so there are rats and
rats. The kind of rats we are *not* interested in here are
the brown and black ones which are at once destructive
to foodstuffs and other things, and spread certain virulent
diseases of man. The kind I shall try to get you interested
in, however, is the *white rat,* or *albino* rat to give it its
proper name, a harmless little fellow that is very tame,
never bites or scratches and is quite as clean as any other
animal if you keep it so, and, it follows, it can be handled
with impunity.

There are two ways that you can make white rats serve
you as a hobby and these are (*1*) by breeding them, and
(*2*) by making experiments with them. It is interesting to
breed them and get a pure blood strain and when you have
done this they will not develop any unexpected variations.
When the baby white rats are born they have no hair on
their translucent pink skins and their *innards* show through
it in dark-colored patches. By the time they are a week
old their bodies are covered with a downy hair and they
are cute, cunning, and very attractive.

White rats are largely used for testing the action of
vitamins in various foods and other substances on them.
If you are interested in making experiments with them to
determine the nutritional values of foods you can get all
of the information you need as to how to start from
Dr. Walter H. Eddy, of Teachers' College, Columbia University, New York City. To start a rattery as a breeding

or an experimental hobby you should read *The Breeding and Care of the Albino Rat,* by Greenman and Dubwing.[9] You can get pure-bred white rats from Dr. Henry H. Donaldson, of the Wister Institute, Philadelphia.

The White Mice Hobby.—*How to Start a Mousery.* —Well, girlies, here is the kind of a mouse you have been looking for, for he will neither bite, scratch, nor squeeze you. You should by all means get acquainted with him, her or them, so that when you go into the African jungle to shoot lions your innate high courage will not take French leave of you and make you run for the nearest tree.

I refer to the *albino mouse,* or rather *mice,* because whenever there is one you may be sure you will find a dozen or more. The family of white mice is really only a variety of the common mouse, but they are as different in disposition as they are in color, since they will not squeal, bite or scratch, and like to be fondled, to run around all over you, and sleep in your pockets.

A cage of them will make a hobby for the kiddies that is as good as a miniature menagerie. You can buy a pair of them and raise them by the dozen, or a dozen of them and raise them by the million. In nearly every town and city you will find some one who has them, and you should be able to get them of any dealer in pets. Just in case you can't, write to Feodor Zanec, who has a pet store at *804* Eighth Avenue, New York City, and he will see that you get them.

[9] Published by the Wister Institute, Philadelphia, Pa.

PART II

Some More Animal Hobbies

The Pigeon Keeping Hobby.—*How to Start a Pigeon Loft.*—There are numerous kinds of fancy pigeons and chief among these are the pouters, the carriers or homers, the fantails, the nuns, the Jacobins, the turbits, the tumblers and the trumpeteers. To breed fancy pigeons is a very fascinating hobby, and to fly carrier pigeons is an exhilarating and exciting sport.

The *pouter* has long legs, slender body, erect carriage and a distendable crop which it can dilate to a remarkable extent—a process that is called *pouting*. The *carrier* or *homing* pigeon is so called because it is employed to *carry messages* and to return home from a distance, and it is also used for flying races. The various other fancy pigeons have qualities all their own and you will find these described in detail in *Pigeon Raising,* by Alice Macleod, published by D. Appleton-Century Company.

Should you decide to start a pigeon loft your first move is to subscribe for either *The American Pigeon Keeper*, published at 725 S. La Salle Street, Chicago, Ill., or *The American Pigeon Journal,* published at Warrenton, Mo. In either of these papers you will find the cards of owners of pedigreed pigeons and who also sell pure-bred cocks and hens. These papers also carry articles on breeding, raising, training and showing pigeons.

To find out what it is all about and to keep up to the times you should also join a *Pigeon Club,* and to learn of the one that is nearest to you write to the secretary of *The National Pigeon Association,* Box 502, Kansas City,

Mo., or to the American Pigeon Club, *40* Wales Street, Dorcester, Mass. If you would like to breed and fly carrier pigeons (see *Fig. 14*), then get *The American Racing Pigeon News,* published at *214* Congress Street, Jersey City, New Jersey, and join either the *American Racing Pigeon Union,* whose offices are at the above address, or *The International Federation of American Homing Pigeon Fanciers, 114* North Luzerne Avenue, Baltimore, Mary-

FIG. 14.—A PAIR OF STREAMLINE RACERS

Two of the birds exhibited at a pigeon show. They are Two Trick Bobby and Two Trick Bob.

land, and you will get all of the information you need, and in a big way.

The Canary Bird Hobby.—*How to Start a Canary Aviary.*—The *canary* is a little bird that belongs to the *finch family,* and in its wild state it was a native of the Canary Islands, Azores and Madeira. It was introduced into Europe in the beginning of the sixteenth century where they became the most popular of all cage birds because of their remarkable talent for warbling. Later on, the best singers were bred in the Harz mountains in Central Germany.

There are numerous breeds of canaries, the best known of which are the rollers, the cinnamons, the warblers, the choppers, the Yorkshires (shown in *Fig. 15*), and the mules. The *rollers* are so called because they sing in rolling or connected beats; the *cinnamons,* because of their brown color; the *warblers,* because of their singing qualities; the

FIG. 15.—THE YORKSHIRE CANARY

choppers, because they break up their song into definite notes, and can, therefore, whistle simple tunes; the *York-shires,* because they came originally from Yorkshire, and, lastly, the *mules,* because they are a hybrid breed, being a cross between the domestic canary and the sistin, or other wild finches.

There are several strains of rollers, such as the *glucke roller* which sings with glucke-like notes; the *water roller,* whose notes are drawn out like running water; the *hollow roller,* whose notes have a hollow sound; the *low voice* roller, whose notes are quite deep, etc. Then there are the *gluckes* proper, and these include the *bell glucke,* whose notes are bell-like; the *water gluckes,* whose notes are liquid-like, etc.

All of these strains can be taught to sing correct clear notes by personally coaching them, but it is much easier to get phonograph records of the master training singers, and these can be bought of B. M. Mai, *414* North State Street, Chicago, Illinois. I might say here, just in case you are not aware of it, that the male roller canaries can be taught to whistle tunes, such as "Rock-a-bye Baby," "Yankee Doodle," "Hail, Hail, the Gang's All Here," etc., either by personal instruction or, better, because it is more accurate and far less tiresome, by means of phonograph records.

When you have decided to take up canary breeding and raising as a hobby, get a little book called *Fundamentals of Raising Canaries* by William C. Daustin, and published by him at *46* Terracina Boulevard, Redlands, California.[10] Your next move is to subscribe for the *American Canary Magazine,* published at *300* Commercial Building, Louisville, Kentucky, or *Bird Lore,* published in Harrisburg, Pennsylvania.

If you want to make rollers your hobby then get the *Roller Canary Journal* and *Bird World,* published by the *Roller Fanciers Corporation,* at Kansas City, Missouri, and, finally, join a canary bird club, a society or an association, the addresses of which you will find in the above named papers. Should your hobby be roller canaries, then your cue is to join the *International Roller Canary Bird*

[10] The price of this book is *35* cents, plus postage.

Association, 602 Central Exchange Boulevard, Kansas City, Missouri.

The Tropical Fish Hobby.—*How to Start an Aquarium.*—Raising tropical fish is one of the major hobbies and at the present time it is at the very peak of its popularity. Indeed, so great is the interest in it that a million dollars' worth of them are sold every year. To be a tropical fish hobbyist on a small scale is cheap plus and easy minus, but to be a successful one in a big way is a *piscis* of another color.

Tropical fish are, as the name indicates, fish of various kinds and breeds that come to us from tropical countries, and their native habitats are fresh-water ponds and lakes. There is a large number of different varieties for you to choose from, and these are of various sizes and widely divergent prices. I can't begin to enumerate all of them, but a few of the chief ones are (*1*) the guppies, (*2*) coral fish, (*3*) Japanese tropical fish, (*4*) scalares, (*5*) swordtails, (*6*) mollies or platies, (*7*) sailfins, (*8*) spenopes, (*9*) *Symphysodon discus*, (*10*) bettas, (*11*) the Yacatans, (*12*) the tetras, (*13*) the Cyclids, or Siamese fighting fish, etc., a few of which are pictured in *Fig. 16*.

To start a tropical fish aquarium on the cheapest and smallest scale you need only to get a *2-* or *3*-gallon glass jar or a bowl, cover the bottom of it with some fine sand and pebbles, put some aquatic plants in it and nearly fill it with some ordinary water. This done go to the *5* and *10* cent store, or to any dealer in pets, and buy a pair of guppies,[11] or whatever kind you can get for *10, 15* or *20* cents a pair and put them into the jar or bowl.

You do not need to ever change the water, but you

[11] These are less than an inch long.

should add a little occasionally to make up for the amount lost by evaporation, and then you should have a glass siphon [12] and siphon out the refuse from the bottom every

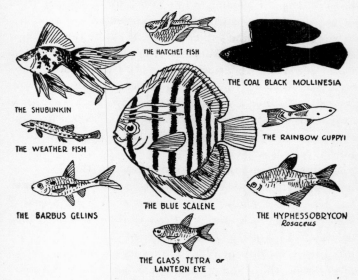

THE HATCHET FISH

THE COAL BLACK MOLLINESIA

THE SHUBUNKIN

THE WEATHER FISH

THE RAINBOW GUPPYI

THE BARBUS GELINS

THE BLUE SCALENE

THE HYPHESSOBRYCON
Rosaceus

THE GLASS TETRA or
LANTERN EYE

FIG. 16.—KINDS OF TROPICAL FISH

once in a while. Keep the water at a little higher than room temperature *all the time,* i. e., between *70* and *75* degrees *Fahrenheit,* and see to it that it never falls below the former point. You can buy food for them for about *10* cents a package which will last a long time.

To make a real hobby of tropical fish, however, you

[12] This is a bent glass tube with two branches of unequal effective length, by which a liquid can be transferred to a lower level. This is done by the pressure of the air on the liquid and forcing it up the shorter branch of the tube that dips in it, while the excess of weight in the longer branch, when once it is filled, causes it to flow continuously.

must learn all about all of the different kinds and how to breed them. As a beginning, send *10* cents to the *Eastern Garden Tropical Fish Hatchery,* Kessena Boulevard and Rose Avenue, Flushing, New York, for a catalogue of their prize-winning specimens. Then you should read one or more books on the subject, and one of the best of these is *Pets* by Christopher W. Coates, Department of Tropical Fish, New York Aquarium, New York City. Another good book is *Tropical Fish,* by W. Ladiges, sold by the *Paramount Aquarium, 24* State Street, New York City. Still another is *Tropical Fish in the Home, Their Care and Propagation,* by F. H. Stoge, sold by Carl Mertens, State Street, New York City.

Then you should take one or more papers that specialize in tropical fish, and chief among these is the *Aquarium,* published in Philadelphia; *Aquarium Home Bulletin,*[13] East Orange, New Jersey; *Penn Fish Culturist,* Philadelphia, and *Aquatic Life,* Baltimore, Maryland. If you live in the vicinity of New York City you should by all means read the column on tropical fish in the Saturday New York *Sun,* which is conducted by Mr. Coates. With this introduction you will have a pretty good idea of what tropical fish are, why, when and how.

The next thing to do is to get a tank, and the larger this is the better, for you will get a greater thrill out of one large aquarium than you will get out of a dozen small ones. A *15*-gallon tank [14] is the smallest size you should get, and if you can afford it buy a *50-* or *100*-gallon one.

[13] A good article for you to read is "The Tyro's Errors," by C. N. Peters, in the *Aquarium Home Bulletin,* in the October, 1934, number.

[14] A tank of this capacity is *12* inches wide, *12* inches high and *2* feet long. The Baskirk Aquarium Company, Independence, Ohio, will quote you prices on all sizes of them.

Put some sand, pebbles and aquatic plants in it, and you will find the names of dealers in these in the various papers I have cited. Nearly fill the tank with water, and to keep it at an even temperature you can fit it with a thermostat and a heater.[15]

Comes now the final and important part of your hobby and that is to catch your tropical fish and this is easy money—that is if you have the money. The cheapest kind is the *guppies,* which cost as little as *10* cents a pair and the costliest kind is the *Cyclids* or *Siamese fighting fish,* which cost as much as *$500* a pair. In between these extremes are the *bettas* which come in all colors and are the acme of beauty, the brilliant red *swordtails,* the black and red-tailed *mollies,* the golden helmet *platies,* the whole family of *tetras,* the Japanese tropical fish, and all of the other tribes too numerous to mention.

Should you have any trouble in getting the kind of specimens you want, write to any one of the above named companies, who are wholesale dealers in tropical fish, and you will get a reply telling you of the nearest dealer who can supply you. Your local dealer will be able to tell you about the club or clubs in your vicinity, and you can find the names and addresses of the various societies and associations that you can join, and where tropical fish shows are to be held, in the various papers I have previously mentioned.

The Bee Keeping Hobby.—*How to Start an Apiary.*—No, Gracie, an apiary is not a place where they keep apes, but bees—you know, those little flying insects of the order *Hymenoptera,* of the super-family *Apoidea,* and of the genera *Apis mellifera*—the kind that makes honey.

---

[15] The Marco Product Company, Bloomfield, New Jersey, make them.

The common honey-bee is believed to have had its origin in Southeastern Asia, and to have been domesticated in Egypt and Greece about the dawn of civilization. Bee keeping found its way into Europe with the invasion of the Romans and it came to America with the early colonists.

There are several races of honey-bees, the chief ones of which are (*1*) the brown, black, or German race, (*2*) the yellow, or Italian race, and (*3*) the gray, or Carniolan race. The black race have mean dispositions, while the yellow and gray races are very gentle and, it follows, they are the kind for you to keep. A *bee colony,* as the bees which live together in a single hive are called, may consist of as few as *200* members, or it may have as many as *60,000* or *70,000* members.

Each colony is formed of three kinds of bees: (*1*) the queen, (*2*) the drones, or male bees, and (*3*) the workers. There is only one *queen* in a colony, and this is a fully developed female; she can, after being fertilized by the male, produce an almost unlimited number of eggs. She is the largest of the bees and the mother of the colony.

The *drones,* or *male bees,* are smaller than the queen; they have no stingers and gather no honey and their only mission in life is to impregnate the queen. The male who does so loses its life, and the other males are often driven from the hive by the *workers.* These latter, who do all of the work of the hive, may number thousands, and these are females whose regenerative organs are so poorly developed they can seldom lay eggs.

How to Start a Hive.—While bee keeping is a simple art, the first thing you should do is to read up on it and so learn a lot of things that will be of help to you. A book that I can highly recommend is *Beekeeping* (*$3.00*) by Emerett Franklin Phillips, Ph.D.[16] Two other good books are *The Honeybee* (*$2.00*) by Longstroth and Dadant, and *First Lessons in Beekeeping* (*$1.00*).[17] At the same time send for the large, free catalogue of *bee supplies* to *The Stover Apiaries,* Tibbee Station, Mississippi, and *The Marshfield Manufacturing Company,* Marshfield, Wisconsin.

Having read the above literature you are ready now to get (*1*) a hive, (*2*) the bees, and (*3*) a state license for bee keeping, if your state requires it, in which case you can get it of the town clerk. The *hive* is simply a box, with hinged sides and a hole in it for the bees to make their entrances and exits, in which *frames* are placed and it is these that the bees fill with honey. Now get a small colony of bees, or *nucleus* as it is called, and this must include a queen. You can buy the bees of some apiarist or apiaculturist who lives near you, or of some of the regular dealers in bees whose names and addresses you will find in the *American Bee Journal,* which I have cited above.

You can keep bees almost anywhere, even in a large city, in which case you put the hive on the roof of the building you live in, or in the back yard, if you have one. Almost any place will do where the supply of nectar [18] is near enough so that the bees won't have to waste too much of their energy in making long flights.

When you get your colony of bees from a distant dealer, they will come in a package, and you can then transfer

[16] Published by the Macmillan Co., New York.

[17] Both of these are published by *The American Bee Journal,* Hamilton, Ill.

[18] This is a sweet liquid secreted by the nectaries of a plant and it is the chief source of nectar of the honey-bees.

them to the hive where they will, in due time, increase and multiply enormously; at the same time they will build up hexagonal wax cells that form the honeycomb and, finally, they will fill these with honey.

One of the most interesting and, withal, exciting features of bee keeping is that of *swarming,* and this takes place when the number of bees in a hive becomes too great and another queen is hatched among them. It is then that a large portion of them with one of the queens, usually the new one, rush like mad from the hive in a body and form a new colony. After flying violently around for a while they will all settle on the limb of a tree in a mass.

When they have done this you must direct them into the new hive which you have ready for them, and this you must place on a sheet wherever you want it to permanently remain. This done, make a dense smoke with a *smoker,* which is an apparatus for making and directing a stream of smoke, and smoke the swarm with it, as this will help to keep them quiet. You can then cut off the limb with the bees on it and lay it on the sheet. It is a good scheme to put a few of the bees in the entrance hole of the hive when all of the others will gradually follow. They will then get busy cleaning it out, making the honeycomb, then flying out for the nectar, bringing it back to the hive and, finally, filling the cells with it.

The Ant Culture Hobby.—*How to Start a Nest.*— Equally as exciting as bee keeping is the study of ants, and it has the advantage over either of the foregoing hobbies of costing you absolutely nothing, but the time you put on it. If, then, you want a hobby that will keep you in the open air and which is not too strenuous, there is nothing more delightful and instructive than to make a field study of these little animals.

To supplement your field study of them, you can transfer a colony from their habitat outdoors to an artificial nest indoors, and there observe their behavior at closer range and without the slightest effort on your part. Before you take up ants as a hobby it would be a good idea to read up on them and you will find the whole story about them in *Ants, Their Structure, Development and Behavior,* by William Morton Wheeler, Ph.D.[19]

Armed with the knowledge you will gather from it you can go as deeply into the study as you may care to. Just in case, however, you might want to make a few preliminary observations to see whether you want to take up ants as a permanent hobby, I'll tell you how to do so.

All you have to do to make a *field study* of them is to get a magnifying glass—a reading glass will do—and then sally forth in the fields and through the woods. You will find nests of them under stones and logs, in bark, rotten wood, in hollow twigs, and about the roots of plants, as well as in the open soil.

To study them at home you must make an *artificial nest,* and of these there are two kinds, namely, those (*1*) with earth and (*2*) without earth. The kind made *with earth* conforms to their natural environment, but that made *without earth* does not interfere with their activities except excavating, which is simply suspended for the time being.

To make a simple artificial nest you need only to put some earth in a dish and set this in a larger dish that has

[19] Published by The Columbia University Press, New York.

some water in it. This will prevent the ants from getting
beyond the confines of their nest. The inside dish should
be covered with a sheet of red- or orange-tinted glass so
that it will keep out the ultra-violet light which they do
not like, and this is the reason they live as much as possible
in the dark.

To collect a colony of ants you will need a strong trowel,
or a short and wide chisel will do, for digging out the nests,
and a large, wide-mouthed bottle to put them in if the
colony is small, or a bag if it is a large one. When you get
them home all you have to do is to transfer them to the
artificial nest when you are ready to observe their behavior. Close observation will reveal some of the strange
habits of these little animals as, for example, making slaves
of other species, cultivating fungi for food, and caring for
aphids [20] which produce honeydew,[21] a delicacy they like
very much.

The nest must have two compartments, one for them to
live in and the other to keep their food in. To supply them
with the latter mix a little sponge cake with some honey,
or molasses, when they will carry it to the food compartment and store it there. They also like a bit of apple and
banana, and are especially fond of the muscular parts of
the larvæ of insects. Give them a little water to drink but
do not let any of it get into the food compartment as it
will make the food moldy, and this they heartily dislike.

The Land Snakes Hobby.—This hobby is a *regular
crawler,* as Robert Louis Stevenson used to say. To most
people snakes are animals to keep as far away from as

[20] These are plant lice.
[21] This is a sweet, honey-like secretion produced by aphids and other
insects.

possible, or, failing in this, to kill them as brutally as the means at hand will allow. Now all of this is dead wrong, for if you will but catch, keep and study them, you will be charmed, for you will find that they are not so far removed from their exalted brother man, since they were both evolved from the same original source, and move along through life with their underneaths very close to the ground.

Snakes can be conveniently divided into three general classes: (*1*) harmless snakes, (*2*) non-poisonous snakes, and (*3*) poisonous snakes. By *harmless snakes* are meant those that do not bite, and are not poisonous. Therefore they may be caught and handled with impunity.

A few of the harmless snakes are the *hognose*, or *puff adder* [22] which has a small, stout body; it dilates and flattens its neck and hisses to throw a scare into you, but that is all. The *garter* or *ribbon snake* is so called because it is lined with yellow stripes. It is very active and full of courage, but it is nevertheless perfectly harmless. The *grass snake* is, as its name indicates, a green snake, and it is of the garter species. The *gopher snake* is a large, burrowing one that has a black color marked with red, and the small *boa constrictor* is about *3* feet long and coils about its prey and crushes it.

The *non-poisonous snakes* are those that bite but which do not secrete a poison and, it follows, they are harmless. Some of these snakes are the *black-snake* or *black* or *blue racer* as it is called. It has a length of nearly *6* feet, and, next to the pilot snake it is the largest of the non-poisonous variety. The *pilot snake*, which is also known as the

[22] It is also called the blowing adder, flat-headed adder, and sand viper.

mountain black-snake, is even larger than the common black-snake; it has a lustrous black color, and some of its scales are edged with white. The *King snake* is quite large and nearly black, and is so called because it is supposed to kill other snakes. The *milk snake* gets its name, not because it gives milk, but because it was supposed to visit milk-houses to get milk to drink. This is also a fallacy, its mission to these places being probably to catch mice which infest them. It is of a grayish color with three series of rounded brown blotches on its body and an arrow-shaped spot on the back part of its head. The *water snake,* which has a length of about *4* feet, lives chiefly in fresh water and feeds on aquatic animals. It has a vicious appearance and a hard-boiled disposition. Its bite is severe but it is not poisonous. Lastly, the *coach-whip snake* has scales on it that are colored and patterned so that it gives it a braided appearance, whence its name.

The *poisonous snakes* are those that bite and inject a venom, i. e., a poisonous matter which they secrete in sacs that are back of their fangs, and this often proves fatal when the object of their attack is man. A few of these snakes are the *moccasin* of the uplands of the southern states, and this is probably a dark variety of the *copperhead.* There are certain non-poisonous water snakes, called *moccasins* in the northern states, that resemble the true moccasin in color but they are not of the same species. The *copperhead* is allied to the rattlesnake, but unlike the latter it has no rattle. It is about *3* feet long and is of a copper-brown color above the transverse, with hour-glass shaped markings. It is quicker and more aggressive than its cousin the rattler and frequents rocky places, near woods and marshes. The *rattlesnake,* of which there are several species, has a series of horny, interlocking joints at the end of its tail, called a *rattle,* which makes a rattling sound when shaken. The *prairie rattlesnake* is about 3 feet long, while the diamond *rattlesnake* is sometimes 6 feet long. Rattlers of all kinds have rather thick bodies with large heads and are of a sluggish disposition. They are not inclined to attack except when they are disturbed or are getting their prey. Finally, the *coral snake*

FIG. 17.—THE HOBBY OF CHARMING SNAKES

is a beautifully red- and black-marked specimen and one that will not stand for any fooling.

The snakes I have described above are all natives of the United States, but if you would a-snaking go to India's coral strand you can get a thrilling specimen of what a venomous snake is. This is the *cobra de capello,* which means the *serpent of the hood,* or just *cobra,* as it is called for short.

Now a hobby, or perhaps it is a business, of some of the *fakirs* is to *charm* the cobra with weird music, when it rises to the striking position, as shown in *Fig. 17;* it then dilates the skin of its neck into a broad hood and sways rhythmically forth and back. Before this charming performance begins, however, the fangs of the cobra are removed, thus making it harmless.

How to Get the Snakes.—Having, now, an idea of how to identify the chief common snakes and knowing something of their main characteristics, you are ready to sally forth and capture a few of them. Hunting snakes and bringing 'em back alive will provide you with a fresh and exciting interest in life and, hence, with an unusual hobby.

I would suggest, however, that you confine your efforts at first to snakes of the harmless variety so that you can get acquainted with their cute little ways. Then you can go after, capture, and study the non-poisonous varieties and if you find you have an abiding love for them, you can tackle the poisonous kinds.

The Things You Need.—There are only two or three things you need to capture snakes with, and these are *(1)* a forked stick, *(2)* a pillow slip, or a bag made of some soft material, and *(3)* a suitcase. The most likely place to find your quarry is the countryside where there are dense growths of underbrush, and along stone walls. Having found your snake get close enough to him to pin him to the ground with the forked end of the stick, and this you do by placing the crotch over him directly back of his head, being careful not to bruise him.

This done get a good grip on him just back of the stick with your fingers, and you can then pick him up, and wriggle and lash around as he may he is powerless to bite you if he should happen to be one of that kind. Now open up the pillow-case, or bag, thrust him in it and tie up the

mouth of it when you can carry him home as is, or put the
bag in a suitcase.

Having brought in your catch put it or them in a cage
or den. This should have a solid bottom, three sides of
glass and a back and top of close-fitting wire netting. Put
a layer of sand on the bottom of it and a dish of water in
it. As snakes like water, you should give them a plentiful
supply of it and see to it that it is changed frequently.
Feed the small ones tadpoles and insects, the medium-
sized ones frogs and toads, and the big, bad fellows rats
and rabbits.[23]

Facts and Fancies About Snakes.—The jaws of the
snake are not pivoted as is the usual procedure in verte-
brate animals but they are, instead, connected with liga-
ments; this arrangement enables it to open its mouth wide
enough to swallow animals that are several times larger
than the circumference of its own body.

The teeth of a snake point backward and this construction, together with the alternate reciprocating motion
of its jaws, enables it to pull in its living food, which it
always takes in head first. Probably the reason it does so
is because the hair of the animal it eats projects back
from its head, and this makes it go down the long stretches
of its stomach considerably easier, and then again it saves
its tail to pick its teeth with. See?

Beware the stories which tell you that the whipsnake
is liable to seize you by the buttonhole and give you a good
lashing in the vicinity of your coccyx; [24] that the milk

[23] The best treatise on snakes is *The Reptile Book,* by Dr. Raymond L.
Ditmars, published by Doubleday, Doran and Company, Garden City,
L. I. You should read it before you take them up as a hobby.

[24] This is the end of the vertebral column in man.

snake is so called because it milks cows, and that the hoop-
snake makes a hoop of itself by taking its tail in its mouth
and rolling along at a goodly speed.[25]

[25] For other curious fancies about these elongated, legless reptiles see
my book *Fun With Snakes,* published by the D. T.'s Publishing Company,
15 Bushmaster Street, N. Y. Books by Dr. Ditmars that will really help
you are *Strange Animals I Have Known, Thrills of a Naturalist's Quest,*
and *Confessions of a Scientist.*

CHAPTER V

THE MANUAL ARTS HOBBIES

IF the work you do for your daily bread is of a mental nature, such as bookkeeping, teaching, office work, etc., the best kind of an indoor hobby for you to ride is one that calls for the use of tools. Now there is an impelling charm about visualizing a thing in your brain and then fashioning it with your hands, and a hobby of this kind will act as a balance wheel for your mental activities and this will, in a large measure, ward off nervous breakdowns and a lot of other ills, that constant concentration along a given line brings on.

I have divided this chapter into three parts, namely, (*1*) wood-working hobbies, (*2*) metal-working hobbies, and (*3*) miscellaneous hobbies. To ride any of them to a happy finish takes a certain amount of manual skill, and you may wonder if you have or can acquire it and get the pleasure and recreation out of it that you are taking it up for. My belief is that if you have a burning desire to use either wood or metal working tools, or to print, or weave, or to blow glass, you have, in all probability, the innate co-ordination of brain, eye and hand to do any of these things well.

About the Wood-working Hobbies.—There are at least six different hobbies that you can ride wherein wood is the medium for physically expressing your ideas, and these are (*1*) whittling, (*2*) carpentering, (*3*) cabinet-making, (*4*) jig or scroll sawing, (*5*) wood-turning, and (*6*) carving.

The Whittling Hobby.—The first of the wood hobbies I shall tell you about is the most dreamy, delightful, and perfectly useless, nay, I may say, foolish one that was ever ridden by mortal man. It is strictly an American hobby, and it was running strong when I was a boy. I regret to say, however, that it has long since fallen into innocuous desuetude (whatever that may mean).

Now whittling has the great merit of requiring not the slightest thought or care whatever on your part and in this respect it has playing checkers beaten a mile. Then, again, only two things are needed for its perfect fulfilment and these are (*1*) a jack-knife with a keen-edged blade, and (*2*) a nice, soft pine stick. Oh, yes, another thing you need is a peaceful place which is in tune with your idyllic spirit.

It is not hard to find this kind of an atmosphere in the good old summertime, for all you have to do is to walk along a nice shady road, sit on a fence under a spreading tree, or recline on the grassy bank of a stream or lake, an' whittle an' dream, an' dream an' whittle.

In winter, the ideal condition for whittling is before a red-hot stove in a country store with a few expert expectorators gathered round it, or at home before an open fire with the family about you—but where these places are to be found in this year of our Lord, I wot not. Oh, for the good old days when men were boys and the wooden Indian waved a friendly greeting with his tomahawk in front of the tobacco store.

I have said that whittling is a useless hobby, but on second thought I take that back, for in the long ago the whittler often used the shavings he made to start the kitchen fire.[1] Some whittlers became very adept with the jack-knife and cut out long chains of wood, interlocking block puzzles, miniature ships which they assembled in bottles, and other curious gadgets—and you can do likewise and thereby gain surcease for your troubled soul.

The Carpentering Hobby.—*Carpentering*, or *carpentry*, which is the same thing, is the ordinary and coarser kind of wood-working, such as cutting, framing and joining lumber. To putter around and do odd jobs, you can get along with a very few tools, i. e., a rule, hammer, try and steel squares, a couple of saws, a couple of planes and a bench. To do real carpentry work, however, you need not only a full set of tools [2] but there are certain things you must know and chief among these are how to use (*a*) the carpenter's rule and (*b*) the carpenter's steel square.

The way to use both of these tools, all about the various woods that are used for carpentering, how to put up a frame building, and many other things a carpenter should

[1] As I am writing this chapter I find there is a use, or perhaps by some it would be considered an abuse, for whittling I had never dreamed of, as the following paragraph from the New York *Times* clearly shows:

"PAIR WHITTLE WAY OUT OF JAIL. Erin, Tennessee (AP).—Houston County jail inmates just keep right on whittling after the cell door clangs shut, Sheriff V. A. Rye explaining that it "gives them something to do." Thursday night the chips were flying as usual. But Friday morning two prisoners had gone. A search revealed a huge wooden key protruding from the lock of their cell door."

[2] You can get these in almost any good hardware store, or of Hammacher, Schlemmer and Company, 13th Street and Fourth Avenue, New York City.

know, are all fully described in my book *The Amateur Mechanic*.[3] Since carpentry will be a hobby with you and not a workaday trade you can spend all of the time you want to on each job to the end that it will be good as you can possibly make it, and the excellence of your work as well as the finished product will give you the pleasure and satisfaction that you are entitled to.

The Cabinet-Making Hobby.—*Cabinet-making* is only a finer and more artistic kind of carpentry. The tools you need for it are practically the same except that they are finer and more accurately set. Among the numerous things that you can make are articles of furniture, and if you are a good craftsman you can turn out far better-looking and more substantial pieces than most of the Grand Rapids stuff that is on the market today.

I know a man who took up cabinet-making as a hobby, and among his first efforts was a duplication of a Chippendale[4] chair. So beautifully made was this imitation it looked like the genuine article; a dealer in antiques made him an offer for it with the logical result that he was soon out of the hobbyist class and into the vulgar manufacturing business, but he still maintains that making period furniture is a hobby with him.

Hardwood is generally used for cabinet-making, such as mahogany, oak, birch, walnut and cherry. In cabinet-making the chief things are to have good judgment, an accurate eye, fine tools and to know how to skilfully use them. There are numerous books that you can get which will tell you all about the art of cabinet-making, and you

[3] Published by D. Appleton-Century Company, New York.
[4] Furniture that was designed by, or designed like that of **Thomas Chippendale**, an English cabinet-maker of the eighteenth century, is called *Chippendale*.

will find a chapter on how to make joints and working drawings in my *Handicraft for Boys*.[5]

The Jig-Saw Hobby.—As you may have gathered from what I told you above, you should have a fair-sized room for a shop and quite a kit of tools to do either carpentering or cabinet-making. Now if you find it hard to get these things, don't be discouraged because there are other kinds of wood-working that you can do which take up very little room and require but few tools. Of these the jig-saw, or scroll saw, as it is also called, is the most popular.

A Cheap Jig-Saw Outfit.—The simplest and cheapest jig-saw outfit that you can get costs in the neighborhood of a dollar. It consists of a steel frame, some saw-blades and an awl. For another half-dollar you can get a jig-saw table, which is simply a board with a V sawed out of one end and a clamp screwed to the other end of it, so that you can screw it to your bench or work table, as shown in *Fig. 18*. To do a good job you should also have a set of scroll-saw files, a pair of jeweler's pliers, a screw-driver, and a small hammer. Finally, you will need some trimmings for boxes such as brass hinges, knobs, French screws, brads, catches, small locks, escutcheons, brass moldings, metal legs, and the like.

If it is your idea to saw out brackets and other fancy gimcracks, you should have some sheet designs, impression paper, and fine, thin wood such as bass, whitewood, Spanish cedar, California redwood, black walnut, bird's-eye maple, mahogany, rosewood, satinwood, tulip or cherry. For all ordinary work, such as glove, stationery and other small boxes, bird cages, clock cases, photo-

[5] Published by Frederick A. Stokes Company, N. Y.

frames, etc., ⅛-inch thick wood is the best, but for brackets, plaques, etc., you should use wood that is ¼ of an inch thick.

Designs in great variety for the above articles, as well as patterns for alphabets, doll furniture, toy steam engines, etc., can be had of H. L. Wild, *171* Avenue A, New York City.

The Power Scroll Saw.—In preëlectric days where something better and faster than the hand jig-saw was wanted a *foot-power jig-saw* was used, and this can still be had, but it has now all but given way to the electric power jig-saw, and since its advent the art has thousands of new and enthusiastic followers.

With a good power scroll saw you can cut out puzzles and do the finest kind of marquetry, as well as heavy work, by which I mean wood that is up to *2* inches thick, and this can be done nearly as fast as you can cut it on a hand-saw.

Then you can cut out intricate designs in sheet metal in a few minutes, and it is especially useful for fine silversmith work. With a *sanding attachment* that is held in the V-jaws of the chuck, you can sandpaper the edges of the wood you have cut in a jiffy, and this does away with the tedious and time-consuming operation of hand-filing. Finally, a metal file can likewise be held in the chuck and with it you can finish the edges of the metal work with neatness and dispatch.

Taking the *Delta scroll saw*,[6] which is shown in *Fig. 19,* you can get a *24*-inch one with a four-speed cone pul-

[6] These and other power wood-working machines described in this chapter are made by the Delta Mfg. Co., *3,775* Holton St., Milwaukee, Wis.

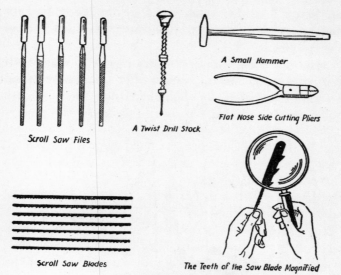

Scroll Saw Files

A Twist Drill Stock

A Small Hammer

Flat Nose Side Cutting Pliers

Scroll Saw Blades

The Teeth of the Saw Blade Magnified

A- THE TOOLS YOU NEED

B- HOW TO USE THE JIG SAW

FIG. 18.—A HAND JIG-SAW OUTFIT

ley, saw blades and wrenches for about *$20.00.* A better
and bigger scroll saw is called the Delta De Luxe, and
the list price of this is *$27.50.* To reduce the vibration,
so that the finest jewelers' blades can be run at the full
speed of the machine the weight of the reciprocating parts
are kept down to the smallest value.

To run the saw you will need an electric motor, and you

Fig. 19.—The Motor Driven Scroll Saw

can get a ¼-horse-power, *60*-cycle, split-phase, *110*-volt
alternating current motor for about *$8.00* additional; or,
better, because it is more powerful, a ⅓ H.P. motor for
about *$13.00;* or still better, because its efficiency is
higher, and takes less current for a given load, a ⅓ H.P.,
repulsion-induction motor for about *$19.00.*

The Wood Turning Hobby.—Another and most
alluring kind of woodwork is *turning,* that is to spin a stick

in a lathe and give it a cylindrical or a spherical shape with a chisel or gouge. To turn up a piece of wood in a lathe and watch it take on the form you want it to have, will give you the keenest pleasure, but turning is usually a supplementary act to other kinds of wood working.[7]

A Cheap Turning Lathe.—The cheapest wood turning lathe you can buy is called the *Companion*, and it is made by the *Miller's Falls Company*, Miller's Falls, New York, and it is listed at *$10.50*. It has a long and a short rest, three turning tools, an *8*-inch face-plate, and a center. The lathe is fitted with a *4*-inch emery wheel without extra charge. A very useful attachment is a circular saw *3* inches in diameter, and a little saw table with a straight-edge guide goes with it. The total cost is about *$1.50* extra. A scroll saw attachment that can be clamped on the lathe-bed can be had for *$3.00* extra. Better and larger foot-power lathes can, of course, be had for more money.

The Power Turning Lathe.—A motor driven turning lathe is as great and glorious an advance over the old foot-power lathe as the motor-driven scroll saw is over the old foot-power scroll saw, and this accounts for the fact that thousands of these lathes are being acquired every year by as many ardent hobbyists.

The cheapest wood-turning lathe that is made by the *Delta Manufacturing Company* is a *9*-inch, *4*-speed, bench lathe, the list price of which is *$19.85*, and this includes a *3*-inch face plate, spur center, cup center, *12*-inch tool support and a pair of wrenches. The Delta *11*-inch, *4*-speed lathe is a good one for you to invest in if you are a serious-

[7] You can get any of the tools described in this section from Hammacher, Schlemmer and Company, *13*th Street and Fourth Avenue, New York City.

minded hobbyist. It is compact, portable, convenient and efficient and one that you can get many happy returns out of. Metal spinning is an enchanting hobby in its own right and you can do it on this lathe to perfection. As a bench lathe its list price is *$28.85* while a lathe stand for it costs nearly *$20.00* more.

The Delta double-duty lathe unit is so called because it can be used for either wood or metal turning. It includes the lathe I have just described and a slide rest. With this combination you can do dozens of jobs that you would otherwise have to let a machinist do for you, or else get a separate metal turning lathe on which to do them.

By having one of these units, an entirely new field of usefulness is opened up to you, for practically everything in the way of metal lathe work, except screw-cutting, can be done on it. The list price of the slide-rest is *$17.85*.

To run the *9*-inch bench lathe, you can use either a $\frac{1}{3}$ or a $\frac{1}{4}$ H.P., *60*-cycle, split-phase, *110* volt alternating current motor, while it is advisable to run the *11*-inch lathe with a $\frac{1}{3}$ H.P., repulsion-induction motor.

The Tools You Need.—Wood-turning tools are simply *chisels* and *gouges*,[8] and both of these have their cutting edges at the ends of the blades. The chisels have flat cutting edges and are made with different shaped points; they can be had in all sizes from $\frac{1}{4}$ to *1* inch wide. The gouges have concavo-convex edges and these are used for cutting channels and grooves. You can buy them of *Hammacher, Schlemmer and Company, 13*th Street and

[8] Buck Brothers' turning tools are largely used by professional wood-turners.

Fourth Avenue, New York City. The way to turn wood is explained in my book *Handicraft for Boys*.[9]

The Electric Workshop Hobby.—Before the small fractional horse-power motor came into use to be a wood-worker required a large expenditure of muscular energy and the pleasure of making things was just a little less than offset by the hard labor that was necessary to produce them. Still the wood-working hobby had its multitude of partisans and these have been increased at least ten-fold since the electric motor provides the power for doing everything that was formerly done by manual labor, as is proved by the numerous makers of small power tools.

All over this great country of ours you will find miniature wood-working shops rigged up in attics, spare-rooms, basements, outhouses and garages, and each of these is presided over by a veritable dictator who leads a Hyde and Jekyll life, being a hard-boiled lawyer, doctor, beggarman, thief, by profession, and a simple, amiable artisan in wood in his spare time.

I have already told you about the power scroll saw and turning lathe, but there are several other machines that you will need if you are bent on having a complete woodworking shop, the chief ones of which are (*1*) a band saw, (*2*) a circular saw, and (*3*) a drill press. The band saw is one in which the saw is made in the form of an endless steel belt with teeth cut in one of its edges, and this runs over a pair of aligned pulleys; it is used for cutting thicker wood and coarser work than can be done with a scroll saw.

A circular saw is one made of a thin steel disk with teeth

[9] Published by the Frederick A. Stokes Company, N. Y.

on its periphery, and this is mounted on a spindle that revolves at a fairly high speed, and it is used for ripping and cross-cutting boards and other lumber. Finally, a drill-press is, ordinarily, a machine for drilling holes in metals, but you can use a Delta triple-duty drill-press for a number of wood-working operations, the chief ones of which are (*1*) boring holes up to *2* inches in diameter, (*2*) mortising square-end holes from ¼ to ½ inches wide and of any length, (*3*) routing out intricate work that would take hours to do by hand, (*4*) shaping the edges of straight and curved work with a minimum of labor and embellishing work that would cost you much time and effort, and, finally, (*5*) smoothing up the edges of work with a speed and accuracy that you could not begin to equal if you sandpapered it by hand.

The Combination Units Workshop.—The unit machines described above can be so combined that the tools are mounted on the same bench or stand. Thus the band saw and mortiser can be combined by mounting them on the same bench or stand with the scroll saw, when they can be driven by the same motor. Likewise the band saw, circular saw and turning lathe can be mounted on the same bench or stand, when they can all be driven by a single line shaft that is connected with the motor. By using the units in combination you have all of your machines directly at hand, and your workshop will take up the minimum of room.

The Wood Carving Hobby.—*Wood-carving* is really more of an art than it is a craft, and it is a hobby that is as pleasing to women and girls as it is to men and boys. It consists of the shaping of designs, adornments and figures with carving tools; it can be used with telling effect in numerous ways and it is one that permits you to express yourself in terms of art.

Now some kinds of wood-carving are quite easy and others are very difficult to master unless you have an inherent gift for doing it. Thus, what is known as *chip,* or *surface carving,* is easy plus; *panel,* or *relief carving* is considerably harder, while *figure carving* requires real genius.

FIG. 20.—THE HOBBY OF CHIP CARVING

When you were a boy and cut your initials on the top of your school desk, or on the side of a fence or a tree, the artistic instinct of your savage ancestors was cropping out. Any kind of carving on a flat surface is called *chip carving* and some of it is very pretty. A young wood-carver is shown in *Fig. 20.*

What is called *panel carving* is also done on a flat piece of wood but the design stands out in relief and this is made by cutting out, or *sinking* the ground. Should you want a part of the design to stand out above the surface you can carve it out of a separate piece of wood and then glue it on, or *plant* it, as it is called, under the pressure of a wood screw. Carving a flower or an animal out of solid wood, or *figure carving*, requires a natural aptitude for art and a native skill for using tools.

The Tools You Need.—For chip carving you can get along with three tools, a ¼-inch chisel, a parting tool which is a V-shaped gouge, and a veining tool, that is used for cutting fine lines and veins. These tools will cost you about $1.00 each. For panel carving you will need the above tools plus a short-bend gouge, a long-bend gouge, and a marker for putting in backgrounds. For figure carving you must have a full set of carving tools, several oilstones with which to sharpen them, a marker, a mallet, a set of rasps and a vise. You can get the complete set of tools including an illustrated book of instructions for $15.00.

There is a mighty good little book called *Wood-Carving,* by T. C. Simmons, that tells exactly how to do wood carving of all kinds. It also describes the different kinds of tools and tells how to use and sharpen them and, finally, it explains all about the different kinds of wood that are used.[10]

About Metal-Working Hobbies.—Metal work can be divided into two chief parts, and these are (*1*) hand metal work, and (*2*) machine metal work. There are several kinds of hand metal work, that is, work which you can do with hand tools, and this can be divided into two subparts, i. e., (*a*) ornamental work and (*b*) practical work.

[10] The price of this book is *$1.50,* and you can get it and the tools from Hammacher, Schlemmer and Company, *13*th Street and Fourth Avenue, New York.

Hand and Bench Work.—Among the former are (a) Venetian ironwork; (b) repoussé work; (c) pierced and sawed brass work, and (d) pewter work. *Venetian ironwork* is a pretty and useful kind of hobby, and it consists of bending thin, narrow strips of wrought iron into scrolls and other shapes, and then fixing them together with little iron clamps, called *binders*. This work is easy to do and you need only a few tools and inexpensive materials to do it with.[11]

Repoussé work [12] consists of hammering out designs in relief on a sheet of copper or other metal. Very few tools are needed for this work but it is important to use the right kind. *Pierced metal work* is by all odds the simplest and easiest of ornamental metal work and you won't need any practice to do a fairly good job. *Sawed metal work* consists of sawing a design out of a sheet of brass or other metal—in other words, it is scroll sawing in which a sheet of metal is used instead of wood.

Casting and working pewter is a fascinating process. Pewter is a very malleable alloy [13] and you can either cast it or you can work it into any shape. There is a beauty and dignity about pewterware that none of the other common metals have, and there are many hobbyists who are making artistic utensils of it. The way in which pewter is usually cast by the amateur is by using plaster-of-Paris molds. To finish flat pewterware such as plates and the like, they are scraped with a steel scraper, while round

[11] All of the ornamental work hobbies cited in this part are explained in detail in my book *Handicraft for Boys*, published by Frederick A. Stokes and Company, New York.

[12] Repoussé (pronounced re-poo-say') is a French word and means *to form in relief.*

[13] Pewter is formed of *25* per cent lead and *75* per cent tin.

objects, such as cups, are turned up in a turning lathe.

By *practical hand metal work* is meant that branch
which belongs to the various mechanics' trades. While
there are several of these the only one that you are likely
to be able to make a real hobby of is machinist's work.
Now there are many things that you can make and do if
you have a few machinist's hand tools, and given these, a
bench, and a suitable room, or place to work, you are ready
to try out the hobby of the amateur machinist.

Power Machine Work.—To get the full measure of
pleasure and satisfaction out of your machinist's hobby
you should by all means have a lathe, and so let's take a
look at the different kinds to the end that you may get
one exactly to your liking.

Now there are three different kinds of lathes and these
are (*1*) the simple lathe, (*2*) the slide-rest lathe, and (*3*)
the screw-cutting lathe. A *simple lathe* is fitted with a
tee rest, and as the tool you are using is held in your hand,
it follows, you cannot do any very accurate work on it.
The *slide-rest lathe* consists of the simple lathe plus a
hand-operated slide-rest. This latter holds the tool rigidly
in position and hence you can do work with it that approximates accuracy.

Finally, the screw-cutting engine lathe (see *Fig. 21*),
has a slide rest that is geared to what is called a *lead screw;*
this carries it along automatically and the work done with
it is one of precision. The simple lathe and the slide-rest
lathe can be operated with a treadle, i. e., by foot power,
or by an electric motor. The screw-cutting engine lathe
can be operated only by electric power, or the power of
some prime mover. Numerous attachments for all of these
lathes can be had and these will enable you to do prac-

tically any job from turning up a pin to building a gasoline engine. These lathes range in price from about *$25.00*
to *$163.00* for a *9*-inch junior bench lathe. This latter
price includes a wall countershaft and numerous other
equipment and attachments, but without the motor.

If you want to make the use of machinist's hand or

FIG. 21.—THE SOUTH BEND 9-INCH "WORKSHOP" SCREW-CUTTING
LATHE

power machine tools your hobby, the first thing you should
do is to get my book called *The Amateur Machinist*.[14]
The first part of it tells all about all kinds of bench tools
and how to use them, and the last part all about the lathe
and the tools, accessories, and attachments that go with
it and how to use it for doing all kinds of jobs.

Miscellaneous Manual Arts Hobbies.—There are a

[14] Published by D. Appleton-Century Company, New York.

number of manual arts that bear no relation to each other but any one of which will make a fine hobby for you to ride. Chief among these are (*1*) printing, (*2*) book-binding, (*3*) weaving, and (*4*) glass-blowing.

The Printing Press Hobby.—Printing is one of the oldest, most intellectual and useful of the hobbies. Ever since Gutenburg [15] invented movable type and printed from them, some *500* years ago, every boy and not a few men have wanted to stick type and run off impressions on a press; many thousands have done so with unalloyed pleasure and with great benefit and behoof to themselves, and you can do likewise if you care to.

The Kind of a Press You Want.—There are two kinds of small printing presses made, (*1*) the hand-inking press, and (*2*) the self-inking press. Now you can make a printing press out of wood [16] but to do a good job you must have one that is built of iron and *machined,* that is properly finished up.

You can get a small press that has a chase *3* by *5* inches, and will print jobs as large as a postal card, for about *$5.00;* one that has a chase *5* by *8* inches that will print jobs the size of a book page, and this costs *$18.00,* while one that has a chase *6* by *10* inches on which you can print a little newspaper or a magazine, sells for *$25.00.* For a *3* by *5* press you can get along with one font of type, some leads, a type case, furniture,[17] and a

[15] Johannes Gutenburg (pronounced $g\overline{oo}'$-ten-berk) lived from 1398 to 1468.

[16] You will find instructions for making one in my book *Making Things for Fun,* published by D. Appleton-Century Company, New York.

[17] By *furniture* is meant pieces of wood or metal which are less than type high, that are placed between or around type that is to be printed and which together with quoins holds it fast in the chase.

can of printer's ink, and this outfit can be had for a couple
of dollars.

For the *5* by *8* press, you should have the above outfit
plus two additional fonts of type and cases for them, a
set of gage pins, a pair of tweezers, or a bodkin, and this
will cost you about *$5.00*. Finally, for a *6* by *10* press you
will need at least four fonts of type, and more if you can

FIG. 22.—THE EXCELSIOR SELF-INKING PRESS

afford it, all of the foregoing outfit, and also a composing
stick, which is a little metal tray to put the type in as
you set it up, and this outfit will cost in the neighborhood
of *$10.00* or *$15.00*. A self-inking hand press is shown in
Fig. 22.

The Jobs That You Can Do.—With a *3* by *5* press you
can print visiting cards, business cards, labels of all kinds,
tickets for festivals, entertainments, and other purposes,

small letterheads and envelops, bill-heads, statements, and anything else that is not over 2½ inches wide and 4½ inches long. With a 5 by 8 press you can do all kinds of job printing, but the greatest pleasure will accrue to you if you will write a story, or a flock of poems, then print them on good heavy paper and bind them into a real book. This is the way that many of the literati of Greenwich Village get their output into permanent form, to the end that their sanguinary efforts shall not be lost to the world, hard-boiled publishers to the contrary notwithstanding.

To print a book, you can set up each page separately and run off as many copies of it as you want books, and when you have them all printed you are ready to lay them up. The next thing to do is to bind them together and put them between covers. You will find the operations of printing and bookbinding simply explained in my *Handicraft for Boys,* and if you will follow the directions I have given, you will be able to bind your book so that you will be proud to show it to all and sundry.

Printing a Paper or a Magazine.—With a 6 by 10 press, you can print a little newspaper or a full-sized magazine, and in either case you will be your own editor, advertising and subscription manager, typesetter, pressman and printer's devil [18] all rolled into one. But if I were in your place, I should not try to get out more than one issue a month, because if you do your hobby will then become real work and instead of getting pleasure out of it you will get a flock of worries.

Where to Buy a Printing Outfit.—For sizes and prices

---

[18] The term *printer's devil* means the boy who does the chores, and who is usually besmeared with printer's ink.

of presses, styles and prices of type for cards, circulars, books and newspaper work, cuts for illustrative purposes, type cases, paper cutters, wire binding machines, and card and paper stock, write to the *Kelsey Press Company,* Meriden, Connecticut.

The Bookbinding Hobby.—*Bookbinding* is one of the classic crafts and it is a hobby that requires time, patience and skill to turn out a job that you can feel proud of. But whatever effort you put on and into it will well be worth your while, for the finished thing will be a joy forever.

If you are going to make bookbinding your hobby, the first thing you should do is to go to a bindery and see how the professional binder does it. As I have mentioned above, there is a section that tells how to bind books in my *Handicraft for Boys,* and as a starter you can use this to go by.

The Hobby of Hand Weaving.—*Weaving* is one of the oldest of the manual arts and it probably had its beginning about the time that prehistoric man began to domesticate animals, or a little before. The same fundamental principles that were used in those primordial days form the basis of the art as it is now practised, albeit many improvements have been made in the equipment. The keen pleasure and great satisfaction you will get out of weaving, especially if you have a creative mind, is out of all proportion to the small amount that the hobby will cost you.

There are a number of hand looms on the market and these range in price from a little one that is made for a toy, but which does really creditable work, and sells for *$5.00,* to a large one that makes a great variety of fabrics, and which sells for *$45.00;* and, of course, there are looms at prices in between these extremes.

Weaving on the toy loom, a picture of which is shown in *Fig. 23,* is one of the finest hobbies for little girls imaginable, and with it they can make scarfs, doll clothes, rugs, hand bags, etc., in fact anything that does not require goods which is more than *4* inches wide. This little

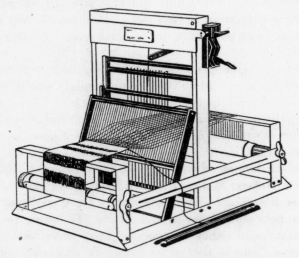

FIG. 23.—THE STRUCTO TOY ARTCRAFT LOOM

loom comes to you completely assembled and threaded with warp, so that there is no delay in starting to weave. Complete instructions go with each loom and also a supply of weft material. It is so simple to operate that a little girl can do a very good job the first time she tries.

The larger and more practical looms can be had in various sizes and with the first of these (No. *240*) you can weave a fabric that is *8* inches wide; this comes with *4* shuttles, filled warp beam, draw-in hook, instruction book and *6* pattern drafts, and it costs *$10.00*. The second loom (No. *420*) will weave a fabric *14* inches wide, has *2* shuttles, draw-in hook, *2* lease rods, unfilled warp beam, instruction book and *9* pattern drafts, and it sells for *$22.00*.

The third one (No. *600*) weaves a fabric *20* inches wide, has the same equipment as the No. *420*, but with *12* pattern drafts, and this is sold for *$30.00*. When this loom is furnished with *8* harnesses, instead of the usual *4*, it sells for *$45.00*. For a complete description of these looms write to the *Structo Manufacturing Company*, Freeport, Illinois, for their *Artcraft Loom and Weaving Accessories* catalogue.

There are two good books you should read on weaving, and these are *The Shuttle-Craft Book of American Hand-Weaving* (*$6.50*) by Mary M. Atwater, one of the foremost authorities on weaving, whose address is *2* Empson Block, Helena, Montana, and the other one is *Foot-Power Loom Weaving* (*$6.00*) by Edward M. Worst.[19]

To be a real hand-weaver hobbyist you should join the *Shuttle-Craft Guild,* an organization which brings its members into close touch with each other and disseminates information about weaving, books, patterns, equipment and provides a complete course of instruction by correspondence. It also issues a monthly news letter called *The Shuttle Craft Bulletin,* and this furnishes the members with the latest information, new patterns and helpful suggestions. There are several teachers of weaving in the United States, and you can get the name and address of the one who is nearest to you

[19] Published by the Bruce Publishing Company, Milwaukee, Wisconsin.

from the *Structo Manufacturing Company,* Freeport, Illinois. Finally, a wide variety of yarns, ready-wound warp beams and weaving supplies can be had from *Emile Bernat and Sons Company,* Jamaica Plains, Massachusetts, and if you will write to them they will send you a price list and color card.

The Glass-Blowing Hobby.—One of the most fascinating of the manual arts hobbies is *blowing glass.* The reason for this is because glass is so hard and yet so fragile it seems to the ordinary observer to be beyond the pale of tools. *Au contraire,* as the French say, it is not at all hard to blow glass if you will but mix your artistic taste with the necessary skill and use the right kind of materials and apparatus.

Now glass-blowing is the art of giving a mass of glass whatever shape you want it to have, and this you do by heating it to a semi-liquid state and blowing it through a tube. There are two classes of objects you can make by blowing it, to wit, those that have (*1*) a useful purpose, and (*2*) an artistic value. The *useful kind* include bulbs, flasks, and the like for chemical and other purposes, while the *artistic kind* are such objects as flowers, animals, and other beautiful things.

A highly specialized form of glass-blowing is the making of large models of various insects such as the flea, mosquito, fly, ant, bee, etc.[20] To make these of glass you must first of all draw enlarged views of them to scale and put in every detail as revealed by a magnifying lens. You are ready then to make them of glass.

[20] If you live in New York City, or visit it, you should by all means see the glass models of insects in *The American Museum of Natural History.* If you are interested in making them yourself, you should see Mr. Herman O. Mueller who makes them for the Museum.

The Apparatus You Need.—The chief piece of apparatus you need is a *blowpipe,* and this consists of two metal
tubes, one inside of the other. The outer tube is connected
with a source of ordinary illuminating gas and the tube
inside of it, which has a glass nozzle in its open end, is
connected with a source of compressed air. The way the
blowpipe is made and connected up is clearly shown in

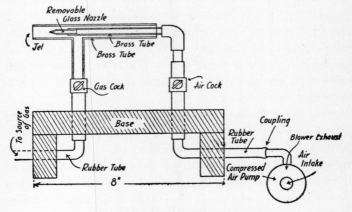

FIG. 24.—HOW THE BLOWPIPE IS MADE

Fig. 24, and you can make one for a dollar or a little
more, with the exception of the equipment for compress-
ing the air.

There are three ways open to you to get the compressed
air and these are by (*a*) connecting the air pipe with the
blower exhaust of a vacuum cleaner, and this you do by
removing the dust bag of it, (*b*) using a foot-blower, and
(*c*) using a little motor-driven air compressor. Since every
home has a *vacuum cleaner* it follows that it will cost you
nothing; a *foot-bellows* will cost you in the neighborhood

of *$10.00*, while you can buy an *air-compressor* for about *$10.00* and the electric motor to drive it with will cost you an additional *$10.00*.[21]

The Materials You Need.—The only tools you need are pieces of charcoal that you have shaved down so that you can *border* the end of a tube, that is, enlarge it, a small three-cornered file, and some fine wire. For blowing glass you must use what is called clear *soft glass* and you can get this in various sizes of Eimer and Amend; and colored glass of Leo Popper and Sons, *143* Franklin Street, New York City.

Your first attempts at blowing glass should be confined to bending a tube of it to different shapes, then to *border* it, next to *seal off*, that is to close in a tube, follow on by joining two tubes together, and, finally, to blow a bulb on the end of a tube. When you are able to do these simple things you will have a pretty good idea of how to make any shape you want of a piece of tubing, and you can then try your skill at making flowers and animals.

The above fundamental operations are clearly set forth in my *Handicraft for Boys,* and you will find the more advanced operations of the art in the *Elements of Glass Blowing,* by Harihara Parames Waran.[22]

[21] You can get the foot-bellows, and air compressor, and other glass-blowing apparatus from Eimer and Amend, Fourth Avenue and *18*th Street, New York.

[22] Published by G. Bell and Sons, Ltd. London.

CHAPTER VI

MODEL-MAKING HOBBIES

THE hobbies I shall tell you about in this chapter belong to the category of those of the manual arts. The difference between the preceding chapter and this one, however, is that in the former I told you how to use various wood- and metal-working tools, and in this one I have explained how to build a number of highly interesting models.

The Hobby of Building Meccano Models.—The word *Meccano* is a registered trade name of a constructional outfit that enables you to build an almost endless number of mechanical models, such as derricks, cranes, bridges, power plants, machines, Ferris wheels, motor cars, airplanes, steam engines, etc., and then there are dozens of other models that you can build from your own ideas, and many of these work like the real ones in that they actually run when you hook them up to a little electric motor. So I say unto you if you want your boy to become an engineer, get a Meccano outfit for him. It is easy to build with one of them for all you have to do is to *count the holes*.

Now there are various kinds of Meccano sets but each one contains a number of straight girders and angle girders, all of which have a large number of equally spaced holes in them. Then there are axle rods, pulleys, gears, couplings, rubber tires, nuts and bolts, snap rivets and all kinds of motor car, airplane and ship parts. **The** sets range in price from a small one that costs *$1.00,* called the *Apprentice Outfit Kit,* and with which you can build a truss bridge, traveling crane (see *Fig. 25*), bench lathe, merry-go-round, and a score of other models.

With a *No. 10* outfit, which costs *$10.00,* you can build a large truck, fast racing car, snappy roadster, motor cars,

FIG. 25.—A CRANE MADE WITH A MECCANO KIT

all with detachable rubber tires, radiators, and other special parts for motor car building. Finally, with a *No. 15 Ship Building Outfit,* which sells for *$15.00,* you can build an all steel ship, that floats and runs under its own power. The outfit includes a hull, deck, mast, rudder and all of the other necessary parts for building various kinds of naval ships. These outfits are made by *The Meccano Company of America, Inc.,* New Haven, Connecticut, and you can get them at any good toy store.

The Hobby of Building Model Houses.—You probably have seen miniature houses made of pasteboard, set

on imitation grassy plots and surrounded by toy trees
and shrubs, as shown in *Fig. 26,* in the windows of real
estate dealers. Whole cities have been built up of pasteboard and toy props, in the way I have described above;
several of these were shown at the Chicago Exposition,
and it required no effort on the part of the observer to
visualize exactly what the real cities look like.

To make a model house of pasteboard is the easiest

FIG. 26.—A PASTEBOARD MODEL OF A COTTAGE

thing you know, it will cost you next to nothing to make
it, you will learn considerable about architecture, and find
it a most agreeable mode of expressing yourself.

There are two ways to make a model house, and these
are by (*1*) copying one that is already built, and (*2*)
drawing the plans for one and then making a model from
them. To learn how to make model houses so that they
will have a real craftsman look, draw a set of plans to a
scale of ¼ of an inch to the foot, and this can be either
a one- or a two-story house, just as though you were going
to build a real one, and mark all of the dimensions on
them.

This done, cut out the floor, walls and roof of pasteboard, and you can do this either with a pair of shears or the point of a sharp knife. You can make the windows by painting them on the walls or, better, by cutting them out and covering the holes with mica, or cellophane. Now paint in the doors, or cut out holes for them and hinge the cut-outs on with bits of muslin. Finally, paint the walls with appropriate colors, and then glue them together; make the roof, glue it on and paint it when your model house is done.

It is a good scheme to make a few plain houses first in order to improve your technique, before you essay to make one of more elaborate design. When you feel that you are able to do a pretty good job then try your hand at making a bay-window, next a porch, after this a cupola, that is a roof having a conical or a rounded form, a hip and valley roof, and so on until you can make a model house of any size or style.

When you have your model house done get a smooth board, say one that is about 20 by 24 inches on the sides —a bread board or a drawing board will serve admirably —and then do a little landscape gardening, to wit, cover it with imitation grass, lay out gravel walks and set out toy trees and shrubbery on it. Finish the job by mounting your house on the plot, and you will have a miniature home that looks as if it were ready to move into.

The Hobby of Building Model Ships.—This is a hobby that has the tang of the sea air in it, and it will transport you back to those olden, golden, adventurous days when ships were made of wood and men were made of iron. To build models of ships that sailed the seven seas in the early clipper days, and before, will prove the most exhilarating and romantic hobby that you can ride, but I fear me only one thing, and that is the finished product of your genius will transform it from a hobby into a paying craft, though that, albeit, will be your good fortune and, not, I allow, overmuch of my business.

Chief among the many famous and historic ships were the clippers *Flying Cloud* and *Sovereign of the Seas*— white-winged creatures both—which were the work of that master-builder, Donald McKay. *The Constitution*, a frigate launched in *1797* and famed for her victories and exploits of the war of *1812*, whipped the French privateers in the West Indies, fought the Barbary pirates when she defeated five of their ships and captured many others; she was the subject of Holmes' famous poem *Old Ironsides*.

The *Mayflower*, which as you have proudly said so many times, was the good ship that your ancestors came over on in *1620* and is shown in *Fig. 27*. The *Golden Hind* was the romantic galleon which was presented by Queen Elizabeth to Sir Francis Drake in recognition of his valor when he beat the Spanish Armada; it was in this ship that Sir Francis circumnavigated the globe, on which expedition he was accompanied by four other galleons.

Then there was the *Spanish Galleon* in which lion-hearted Spaniards in armor stalked her decks the while guarding the spices and gold in her hold. The Barbary pirates' *Felluca*, a fast lateen-rigged vessel which scoured the Mediterranean in search of Venetian, Spanish and Portuguese ships, and plundered them. The *Viking*, a fantastic black galley with a single sail and many shields, and in which the valiant Norsemen sailed from Scandinavia to Iceland, and even to the shores of America; and, lastly, the *Chinese Junk,* an Oriental ship having bluff lines, high poop and overhanging stem, little or no keel, and pole masts which carry sails with battens running

Fig. 27.—The Mayflower

clear across them. These then are the outstanding ships you can build models of and this is the way to do it.

How to Build the Models.—The first thing to do is to send to *Roy Hancock, 323–325* Douglas Avenue, Portsmouth, Virginia, and get his catalogue of ship models,[1] the price of which is *15* cents. This booklet describes in detail the materials you need to build any of the forego- ing ships and gives the prices of the various parts that go to make up each ship. If you want to make all of the parts of the ship that you are going to build yourself, you can get working drawings (blue-prints) of any of the above models that give you all of the dimensions, for *$1.00* or less.

Roy Hancock also sells good, clear kiln-dried woods such as silver spruce, white pine and basswood for building the hulls and round sticks for making the masts, yards, booms, bowsprits, etc. Also beading and finishing strips of white wood, birch veneer that holds its shape, does not split, is waterproof and can be stained any color; boxwood for blocks, fife-rails, and catheads, and, lastly, rattan, which when heated can easily be bent and will hold its shape; it is used for beading the stern of the hull, and for poop and monkey rails.

To save you the trouble of gluing up the lifts you can get the hull of any ship you want to build cut exactly to line, sandpapered nice and smooth and already for setting the masts. While it is not at all hard to build a ship from a set of blue-prints with the help of the instruction sheets that go with each kit, still it is much easier to do so

---

[1] The Ideal Aeroplane and Supply Company, *17–19* West *18*th Street, New York City, also make a line of kits for building small models of famous ships, that sell for *25* cents and larger ones for *$1.50*.

The Boucher Playthings Mfg. Corp., *126* Lafayette St., New York, also carry a fine line of them.

Paul K. Guillow, of Wakefield, Mass., makes little boat construction kits of the *Mayflower, Norseman,* etc., that sell for *10* cents, and you can get these at stationery stores.

when you have a detailed description of each part and the way to put the various parts together.

Popular Mechanics, Chicago, Illinois, publishes a book called the *Sovereign of the Seas,* the price of which is *$1.00,* that shows in line drawings and working diagrams every stage of the construction of this ship and the clear text tells you the exact size and shape of every piece and how the parts are put together and decorated.

If you are going to build the *Mayflower,* you will find complete working drawings and a clear description of the parts, how to put them together and to embellish them, in my book *Making Things For Fun.* There are several other good books on the subject of model ship building, and you can get a list of these from Roy Hancock.

The Hobby of Building Wagon and Coach Models. —Building models of stage-coaches and covered wagons are in high favor with hobbyists who love to make things. The models are much easier to build than the ships I have described for the very good reason that a smaller number of parts are used and, it follows, the model as a whole is not so intricate. The four chief vehicles are (*1*) the Imperial stage-coach, (*2*) George Washington's private coach, (*3*) the Diamond tally-ho coach, and (*4*) the covered wagon, or prairie schooner.

You can build the *Imperial Stage-Coach* of the Royal Family of Great Britain, which is pictured in *Fig. 28,* in a single evening provided you get a kit with all of the parts cut out and ready to put together. The complete set of parts will cost you about *$5.00* including the working drawings and instructions. Or, if you want to make the parts yourself, you can get a set of full-sized working drawings for *$1.00.* The finished coach will be *6¾* inches wide, *9½* inches high and *18½* inches long, and when placed in your library it will lend a new interest to the glamorous past.

George Washington's Private Coach is a very smart model and it is truly aristocratic in its Colonial simplicity. You can get all of the parts cut out and ready to put together with working drawings and full instructions for about *$5.00*. The overall length of the coach is *20* inches.

FIG. 28.—THE IMPERIAL STAGE-COACH

An additional *$5.00* will bring you a pair of lifelike horses which are fully finished and ready for you to paint. When you have done so, you can hitch them to the coach and then mount them on a base.

The Diamond Tally-Ho Coach is a very perfect reproduction of the early stage-coaches which carried the wayfarers over the plains and mountains before the coming of the railroad. You can get working drawings of it for *$1.00* and make the parts yourself, and you can get a kit with all of the parts ready to put together for about *$5.00*.

The Covered Wagon, or Prairie Schooner as it came to be known, was a long canvas-covered wagon that was used by the pioneers for crossing the prairies. You can get all of the parts made of hardwood and ready to put together for about *$5.00*. When the model is completed it will be *13½* inches high and *23½* inches long and looks exactly like the real thing. The plans, instructions, and parts of all of the above vehicles can be had from *Roy Hancock, 323–325* Douglas Avenue, Portsmouth, Virginia.

The Hobby of Building Model Airplanes.—Building model airplanes is, by long odds, the most popular hobby at the present time of mechanically inclined boys. Now there are two kinds of model airplanes, and these are (*1*) replicas of the big airplanes that are intended only for decorative purposes, and (*2*) models of real airplanes, and which, like them, will fly. The materials for both of these kinds of airplanes are put up in kits with full-sized working plans and simple, clear and easily followed instructions.

The first thing to do if you want to build either kind of the above airplanes is to send to the *Ideal Aeroplane and Supply Company, Inc., 17–19* West *18*th Street, New York City, and to the *Selley Manufacturing Company, Inc., 1377* Gates Avenue, Brooklyn, New York, for their catalogues and price lists of the various kits they put up and parts they make. If you want to make a little flying model, or a larger flying model of either a monoplane or a biplane, you will find drawings and instructions for doing so in my book, *Aviation and All About It*.[2]

How to Build Replica Model Airplanes.—You can go

[2] Published by D. Appleton-Century Company, N. Y.

into almost any stationery or toy store and buy a little kit for making any one of eight little replicas of famous airplanes, called *Shelf Models,* and these will cost you the astounding price of *10* cents each. In case your toy dealer or stationer doesn't keep them in stock, you can get them from the *United Model Airplane and Supply Company,* Irvington, New Jersey.

Each kit includes a block of balsa wood for making the fuselage, a thin sheet of balsa wood on which is stamped the outline of the wings, the stabilizers, pants and the wheels. There are, also, two cakes of paint, one of orange with which to paint the wings and stabilizers, and one of olive drab for painting the fuselage and the tail. There is also a tube of cement with which to fasten the parts together and, finally, a tin propeller. These little airplanes are easy to build, and while they bring out of the boy his ability to construct things, they are at the same time highly entertaining and, it follows, they will provide a hobby that little Willie will spend hours of his restless time on.

The *Ideal Aeroplane and Supply Company* make replica airplane model kits in two sizes and there are *24* famous planes for you to choose from, including the *Lockheed Vega,* the *Travelair,* the *Curtiss Hell Diver, Sopwith Camel,* etc., and you can get any two of the *6*-inch size for *50* cents, plus *10* cents for postage.

The *Selley Manufacturing Company* make a model kit for a replica of Lindbergh's *Blue Bird,* and this sells for *$1.25.* It has a wing span of *15* inches and, hence, it makes a beautiful decorative display model for your mantel, bookcase, radio or den. It takes but a very little time to assemble any one of the above replicas, and you can paint them so that they will look like the original planes, or to suit the dictates of your own fancy.

The bodies of all of the above mentioned airplanes are carved from solid balsa blocks, and all flat surfaces, such as the wings, tail assembly and struts are cut from balsa sheets, as are the landing gears. Finally the miniature wheels or pontoons, whichever the plane calls for, are furnished with the kit. So all you have to do is to cut them out with a sharp knife, sandpaper them smooth, and cement the pieces together. The propellers are two- and three-bladed ones and, in the smaller-sized models these are of stamped aluminum, while in the larger-sized ones they are made of die-cast aluminum.

How to Build Flying Model Airplanes.—To build models of airplanes that will fly, your cue is to again get the price lists of the Selley and the Ideal Aeroplane Companies, when you can then pick out the one you would like most to build. The chief flying models of the Selley Company are (1) the Boeing Transport 247, (2) the Stinson Reliant, (3) the Howard Racer *Pete,* and (4) the Curtiss Swift *XP934.*

Each one of these model airplanes has a wing span of 18 inches and the kit for making it costs 50 cents. Each kit includes a finished wood propeller, stamped balsa wood sheet, colored Jap tissue, rubber cement, wing adhesive, music wire, colored insignia, full-sized plans, building instructions, and everything else that is needed.

The principal flying models of the Ideal Company are (1) the Boeing *P-26A,* (2) the Curtiss Goshawk, and (3) the Stinson Reliant. These are all extra-large super-detail models, they are beautiful to look upon and are marvelous fliers. The *Boeing P-26A* weighs about *2½* ounces, has a wingspan of *21¼* inches, is made exactly to a scale of ¾ of an inch to the foot, and the kit complete will cost you *$1.75*. The real *Boeing P-26A* is considered the most advanced type of all of the fighting planes. It is very fast and with full armament it can do *240* miles an hour. The greatest pleasure will be yours when you build it and you will learn a lot about the principles of aviation,

FIG. 29.—A MODEL OF A 4-PASSENGER AIRPLANE THAT FLIES

and when you fly it—oh boy!—you'll get the thrill of a lifetime out of it.

The *Curtiss Goshawk* weighs *3⅛* ounces, has a *23⅜* inch wingspan and is made exactly to a scale of ¾ of an inch, and the kit is yours for *$2.00*. The big Curtiss plane is a snappy Navy fighter, has a specially designed stream-lined drag ring, two detachable blade propellers, and all of the parts of the model are coated with a high luster finish, with silver, yellow, red and black coloring. Everything is included in the kit so that you can go right ahead and build one of the finest flying planes you would care to own.

The *Stimson Reliant* weighs 3½ ounces, has a wingspan of *32⁵⁄₁₆* inches and is made exactly to a scale of ¾ of an inch to the foot, and the kit complete costs *$3.50*. It is a beautiful, big model and one that you will be proud to have and to fly, as it is an exact reproduction of one of the latest *4*-passenger cabin planes, as *Fig. 29* clearly shows. You'll find several unusual features in this plane, to wit, it has adjustable speed arresters built into the wings, movable cabin doors, seats and control column and other super-detail features. It is gloriously colored in yellow and black and makes a stunning appearance especially when she is in the air.

All of these planes were designed by experienced aircraft men and they have laid out the plans in a way that is so simple, accurate and complete that you or any other boy can build them without the slightest trouble.

The Hobby of Building and Sailing Model Yachts. —This is a two-in-one hobby, for you not only have the quiet pleasure of building the yacht, but the thrilling fun of sailing it. Now there are two ways open to you to build a model sailing yacht, and these are (*1*) to make all of the parts yourself and assemble them, and (*2*) to buy the various parts ready made and then assemble them. Whichever way you do it you can get everything you need from the *Boucher Playthings Manufacturing Corporation, 126* Lafayette Street, New York City.

The Construction Kits.—The lowest priced model sailing yacht construction kit that the above named company puts out is the *Star Combination Kit,* which is shown at

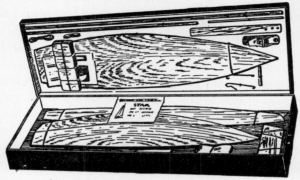

A - THE STAR COMBINATION KIT

B- THE YACHT READY TO SAIL

FIG. 30.—THE STAR MODEL SAILING YACHT

A in *Fig. 30,* and the price of it is *$5.50*. It is a most complete and accurate kit, including, as it does, all of the necessary material cut to the proper size and shape, and, it follows, it is ready for you to assemble; it also contains fully illustrated instructions, a plane, sandpaper and the necessary brads and screws.

The fittings are of nickel-plated brass, and all you have to do is to put them on. The Boucher patent sail shifter is also included in the kit. The yacht, (see *B*), when finished, has a hull length of 28 inches, an overall length of 49 inches, a beam of 7 inches, a draft of 6 inches, a sail area of 404 square inches, and it weighs 3¾ pounds.

The *Carlew Manual Training Kit* was primarily designed to develop the skill of the hobbyist as a craftsman, and it costs *$7.50*. It contains a white pine hull, sawed to the exact outside dimensions and with form templates of it. It also includes the deck, deck beams, keel, spars, rudder, fittings, rigging and a complete set of blue-prints.

To enable you to build a perfectly balanced model, the hull block is laid up with waterproof glue in which a little charcoal has been mixed so that a black line always clearly shows for the exact center and the water line. The building of this yacht will give you a real insight into model yacht construction.

Sailing Models of International Racing Yachts.—The Boucher Company also makes complete construction kits of the famous international racing yachts, the *Enterprise* and the *Shamrock V*, to a scale of ⅜ of an inch to the foot. These sets consist of a hull glued up in layers and this is cut to shape and ready to finish; it is made of the very best grade of California white pine.

Included in each kit, which costs *$25.00*, is the keel, and bolts to secure it to the hull, nickel-plated brass fittings for the above deck, masts and spars of straight grained spruce, and sail cloth cut to shape and ready for finishing. The dimensions of the completed yachts are:

	Enterprise	*Shamrock V*
Overall length	*45* in.	*45* in.
Water line length	*30* in.	*31* in.
Beam	*8½* in.	*7⅞* in.
Height of mast	*56* in.	*56* in.

The *Albatross* is a beautiful sailing model yacht as *Fig. 31* clearly shows. She has powerful lines and a large spread

FIG. 31.—THE SAILING MODEL YACHT *Albatross*

of sail. You can make her either sloop rig or schooner gaff rig. The former is the fastest, but model yachtsmen often prefer the schooner rig because she represents a real sea-going yacht, but whichever rig you use you can sail her in the open water. The dimensions of the *Albatross* are:

Length of hull	50 in.	Draft	9 in.
Beam	11 in.	Sail area	1500 sq. in.
Length of water line	36 in.	Weight	19½ lbs.

The construction kit of the sloop rig yacht is listed at $50.00, and that of the schooner gaff rig is $60.00; or, if you prefer to buy the yacht ready to sail, then the former will cost you $100.00 and the latter $120.00.

The Boucher Speed Boat Construction Kits.—If you

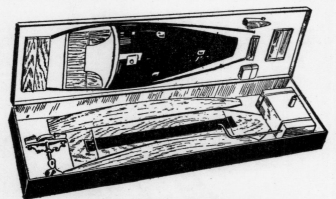

FIG. 32A.—THE POLLY WOG CONSTRUCTION KIT

are a mechanically minded hobbyist and a model boat hobbyist in the same breath, you will sit pretty on the top of the world if you build and run a model motor boat. The Boucher Company puts up several speed boat construction kits, the first one of which is called the *Polly Wog*.

1. You can get a kit for building her hull for $3.00, and this includes the sides of it made of white pine sawed to the finished shape; a bottom of 3-ply waterproof veneer and a stem-piece and transom of mahogany. The deck is of

aluminum, and brads, glue and instructions for assembling her are also included. When finished she has a 7¾-inch beam, and an overall length of *24* inches. The kit is shown at *A* in *Fig. 32.*

2. An outboard motor operated by a little steam boiler (see *B*), for running the boat, has aluminum cylinders, and also gear housing and propellors; the frames, gears and shaft tube are of brass, while the piston rods and flywheel are made of steel. The boiler is formed of seamless drawn

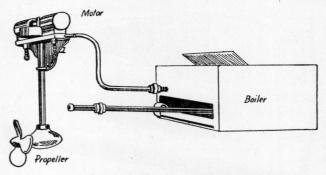

FIG. 32B.—THE OUTBOARD MOTOR UNIT

tubing, and it burns Sterno, or other solidified alcohol. It can be bought for *$10.00.*

Or, if you prefer, you can get the *Polly Wog* powered with the above outboard motor unit complete and ready to run, as pictured at *C*, for *$15.00,* and it will scoot through the water at a high speed for *20* minutes or more, on a single charge of alcohol.

The Boucher Company makes other and larger speed boats and marine power units and you can get these already built, or the construction kits, to build them with, as may be to your liking. The company also carries a beautiful line of 1-, 2-, and 4-cylinder, single- and double-acting marine engines, model boat fittings, books on model boats and boat building, tools, etc.

FIG. 32C.—THE POLLY WOG RARIN' TO GO

Write for a free copy of the *Boucher Blue Ribbon Hobby Book,* which not only lists their various model boats, but gives, as well, practical directions for sailing miniature yachts.

CHAPTER VII

THE FINE ARTS HOBBIES

THE term *fine arts* is used to mean those arts which have for their purpose (*1*) the creation of the finer things of the imagination, and (*2*) the appreciation of their beauty without regard for their utility. By common usage the fine arts include (*a*) drawing, (*b*) painting, (*c*) architecture, and (*d*) sculpture, but in this chapter I have somewhat enlarged the scope of it by adding engraving, etching, photography, modeling, taxidermy, and a few other things.

The Hobby of Drawing.—*Drawing,* as you well know, means a design or a picture that you make with a pencil, pen, crayon, or the like. What we call a *sketch* is a rough or preliminary drawing. A *free-hand drawing* is one that is made by the eye and hand alone, i. e., without the aid of a rule, compass or other instrument, and an *architectural* or a *mechanical drawing* is one that is made with the aid of instruments.

The Sketching Hobby.—To be able to make a sketch of anything you see, that is, to draw a picture of it in free-hand, is one of the nicest, most satisfying and inexpensive hobbies that you can have, for all you have to do is to carry a pad of sketching paper and a pencil with you and do it on the spot.

If you have a natural bent for free-hand drawing, you can make sketches of objects and landscapes that are just as interesting as photographs of them, and which have what they have not, and that is character and individuality. If you haven't the talent for drawing, you can acquire it by practice, for the primitive instinct of expressing yourself by drawing pictures is yours by inheritance, though it may be so dormant you can't recognize it.

To learn to do free-hand drawing is not at all hard if you start in right and I have explained an easy way by which you can draw faces and figures in my book *Handicraft for Boys*. By following these instructions you will be able to succeed marvelously well in getting the right proportions of anything you want to draw. I have also explained in the above named book how to sketch *still-life objects*, that is, inanimate things, such as a cup and saucer, a vase, etc.

Drawing in Perspective.—A *perspective drawing* is one in which the object or view is drawn on a sheet of paper exactly as it is seen by the eye. As an example, if you look down a long street you will see that the roadway appears to be the widest at the place where you are standing and then it gradually gets narrower until it comes to a point and *vanishes* in the distance. The purpose, then, of perspective drawing is to make the object or view stand out in relief just as it does in nature.

In drawing architectural and mechanical subjects and landscapes you must, it follows, know how to draw in perspective. Now there are two kinds of *perspective* drawing and these are (*1*) true perspective drawing, and (*2*) isometric perspective drawing. *True perspective drawing* is the kind that you use when you are drawing buildings and landscapes, and to do this you make use of what are called *vanishing points,* that is all of the lines of them that are parallel to the direct radial appear to the eye to recede from it indefinitely and to meet at the center of vision as shown at *A* in *Fig. 33.*

FIG. 33A.—HOW TO DRAW IN TRUE PERSPECTIVE

Isometric perspective is often used in drawing pictures of machines and the like, and it also makes them stand out in relief, but there are no vanishing points (see *B*), and this makes them very easy to draw. This kind of perspective drawing is purely mechanical and, hence, it is not in

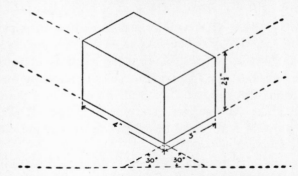

FIG. 33B.—HOW TO DRAW IN ISOMETRIC PERSPECTIVE

the least artistic, but it is very helpful when you are making things for you can draw the lines to scale and still see how they will look when they are finished. The way to make the above kinds of drawings is also described in my *Handicraft for Boys.*

The Tools You Need.—To make architectural and mechanical drawings you will need some drawing paper, a couple of lead pencils, a rubber eraser, a bottle of India ink, a few thumb tacks and a drawing board, also a set of drawing instruments which will include a pair of dividers, a pair of compasses, a ruling pen, a rule or scale, a protractor, a T-square, and, lastly, a *30*-degree triangle. You can get a set for as little as *$1.50* or a better set for *$50.00,* which, of course, will have more and better tools in it.[1]

Some Simple Aids to Drawing.—An easy way to make isometric perspective drawings is to use *isometric drawing paper.* This consists of three series of parallel diagonal lines ruled on it that are *30* degrees apart. You can make it on your drawing board with a T-square and *30*-degree triangle, or buy it ready to use of any dealer in drawing materials.

My book *Handicraft for Boys* also tells how to make simple working drawings, how to draw circles, spirals, and ellipses without tools, how to make and use a *pantograph* for copying, enlarging and reducing drawings, how to make tracings, and, finally, how to make a reflecting drawing board for copying pictures and making original drawings of flat objects. An easy way to draw pictures of objects, landscapes, etc., is to use a little optical instrument called the *camera lucida,* and this is described in my book *Experimental Optics.*[2]

The Silhouette Hobby.—A *silhouette* is a profile, or side view, of the head of a person cut out of black paper

---

[1] For all kinds of drawing materials and tools write to Keuffel and Esser, *127* Fulton St., N. Y.

[2] Published by D. Appleton-Century Company, N. Y.

and mounted on a white card so that it looks like a miniature shadow of the sitter, as pictured at *A* in *Fig. 34.* It got
its name from Etienne de Silhouette, French Minister of
Finance in *1759.* He practised such strict economy in the
conduct of his government's affairs that everything which
was cheap was called by his name. Since photography had
not been discovered and painted portraits were expensive,

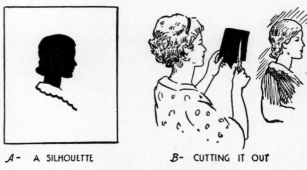

A-   A SILHOUETTE   *B-* CUTTING IT OUT

FIG. 34.—HOW TO CUT OUT SILHOUETTES

the black paper outlines were the cheapest substitute for
portraiture and, hence, his name was given to it.

Today, every one loves these old-time silhouettes, and
if you have the slightest artistic temperament you can
learn how to cut them out with a little practice so that they
will bear a recognizable resemblance to those who sit for
you. I have a friend who cuts out her relatives and
friends, pastes them in an album and labels them, and I
must say it is one of the most unique and lovable hobbies
I have yet come across, besides having the added merit of
being *à la Silhouette,* by which I mean very inexpensive.

How to Cut Out Silhouettes.—All you need to cut out

silhouettes is a pair of scissors and a sheet of glazed paper.[3] Cut it up into pieces about 2 inches wide and 3 inches long and place the sitter so that the side of his or her face is toward you. Now with the paper in your left hand and the scissors in your right hand (see *B*), you begin to cut it at the chin and go on up the profile to the hair; then cut on around to the back of the head and, lastly, down to the collar, and back to the chin again.

As you are cutting it out keep your artistic eye on the profile of the sitter and your mechanical eye on your shears, and you will be not a little surprised to find how small an amount of skill it takes to make a fairly good likeness.

The Hobby of Engraving.—*Engraving* is the art, act and process of producing lines, characters and designs on various hard substances, by cutting into the surface of them with sharp-pointed tools, called *gravers*. *Metal engraving* is used for (*1*) the embellishment of the surface itself, as of silver and gold plate, and (*2*) for producing an original picture or design on a metal plate which can be printed on paper, as stationery, etc. *Wood engraving* is used for producing characters, designs, lines, etc., on blocks of wood for ordinary printing.

The Hobby of Metal Engraving.—Engraving on metal is a beautiful art and a most satisfying hobby. While the process is at once simple and the effects striking, it takes, nevertheless, a good deal of patience and loving practice to do a satisfactory job. Metal engraving is a very inexpensive hobby, for about the only things you need are half a dozen *gravers*, an oilstone to sharpen them on, an eye magnifying glass, and an engraver's pad on which to rest

[3] You can get this at a stationery store, or of the Dennison Mfg. Co., Fifth Ave., and 26th St. New York City.

the work you are going to engrave.[4] All of these are shown at *A* in *Fig. 35,* and the way to hold the graver is pictured at *B*.

To practise metal engraving you can use thick, rolled sheet copper that is planished on one side. The way to hold the gravers and to use them is simply and clearly described in my book *Handicraft for Boys.*

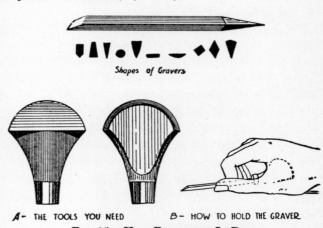

Shapes of Gravers

A - THE TOOLS YOU NEED   *B* - HOW TO HOLD THE GRAVER

FIG. 35.—HOW ENGRAVING IS DONE

Engraving on wood is an art that has quite a large following, and it is one of the most delightful hobbies imaginable, especially if you have a press and do your own printing. The tools you need are the same as those for metal engraving plus a couple of small gouges for cutting away the wood between the lines.

Wood engravings, or just *cuts* as they are called for short, are usually done on blocks of either boxwood or

[4] You can buy engraving tools and accessories of the Jewelers' Supply Co., or of the Anchor Tool and Supply Co., both of which are at *12* John Street, New York City.

maple,[5] and these are exactly as high as ordinary type;
they are sawed across the grain so that your graver will
cut the surface in any direction with equal facility. In making a woodcut you draw the design or picture on the polished surface of the block, and then cut the wood away all
around the lines or spots which are to print so that the
latter will take the ink. You then print from it exactly as
you do ordinary type.

The Hobby of Etching.—The word *etching* means
two things: (*1*) the process of etching, that is, eating a
design or picture into a sheet of metal, or *plate* as it is
called, which is usually of copper, by some corroding
chemical, such as nitric acid, and from which a print is
made, and (*2*) the print so made itself.

To make an etching is a very simple process, but to
make a good etching, that is a print from it, you must have
a lot of artistic ability in order to draw the picture on the
plate,[6] a temperament *à la* Whistler and, finally, a fine
technique, and this is the reason etching is a high-toned
hobby.

The first step in making an etching is to coat the polished surface of a copper plate with a film of acid-resisting
varnish, usually made of asphaltum, wax, and Burgundy
pitch melted together, and then flowed over it. The varnish,
or *etching ground,* or just *ground* for short, is then covered
with soot made by burning a piece of paper under it when
it unites with the other substances. The design or picture
is then traced on the surface and cut through it with a steel

[5] You can get boxwood and maplewood blocks of J. Johnson and
Company, *125* Fulton Street, New York.
[6] There is an easier way, and this is by transferring the design or picture from a sheet of paper to the plate.

sewing needle or other sharp point when the copper lines are exposed.

Nitric acid or hydrochloric acid is next applied to the lines and as the ground resists the action of the acid the copper is eaten away, or etched, when the lines are cut in, in very much the same way as when a graver is used. This done, the ground is removed with kerosene and the surface is wiped off perfectly clean.

The next step is to put a special kind of ink on a dabber and then dab it on to the plate and into the lines. The ink is now carefully rubbed off of the surface, when it (the ink) is left only in the lines. The inked-in etched plate is now laid on the bed of a hand press, a sheet of damp paper is laid on the surface of it and the roller is moved over it; this presses the paper into the etched-in lines, which transfers the ink in them to it. The paper is then pulled from the plate, and an impression of the design or picture is made on it and your etching is done. A very good book that will tell you all about the process of making etchings is the one by B. S. Hammerton, the title of which is *A Treatise on Etching*.

The Hobby of Painting.—Painting is one of the oldest of the fine arts, as is evidenced by the pictures of various mammals found on the walls of the caves at Dordogne, France, and Altamira, Spain, and which were made some *20,000* years ago by *Homo-sapiens,* the nimble-witted man. The desire to paint is, therefore, innate in modern man and, it follows, it is but natural that he should sometime in his young life want to try it as a means of expressing himself.

Just as some individuals have a genius for music, for modeling, and for writing poetry, so, also, some of them have a natural bent for painting and the way for you to find out if you are one of them is to try it. One of the first indications that you have the ability to paint crops out when you find you are constantly scanning pictures in magazines and those in art galleries and comparing them with what you see in nature.

To be a painter you must have (*1*) a good eye for proportion, (*2*) know how to draw in perspective, (*3*) be able to shade correctly, and (*4*) understand the value of colors. An eye for proportion is one that you must naturally have; you can easily learn to draw in perspective; also acquire the knack of shading, and likewise learn how to mix your colors to give them any tint you want.

How to Begin.—Before you try to put colors on a canvas you should practise sketching figures on paper in either pencil or charcoal and shading them in three mediums, namely, shadows, half-tones, and high-lights. When you can do this well, you can then paint the figures in black and white, that is in flats, and practise putting in the shadows, half-tones and high-lights.

In beginning to paint start with simple objects to get the right values. A good way to do this is to set two objects, say a cup and a saucer, in such a way that their lines will overlap for composition. In composition the shadows of the object on one side of the picture must be connected with the shadows on the opposite side of it. In the still-life picture shown at *A* in *Fig. 36* the shape of the shadow is a reversed L, thus ⌐.

The light must come from the upper left side as indicated by the arrow. Those parts of the object against the light should have sharp outlines, while those parts of it against the shadows should be diffused, obscure and verge

with the shadows of the background. When you are satisfied with your work in still-life you can then attempt
to do a head in three tones, i. e., shadows, half-tones and
high-lights, as pictured at *B*.

The letters I have marked on the head are *S* for shadows, *HT* for half-tones, and *HL* for high-lights. The next
step is to practise blending the lights and the shadows

A- SHADING STILL LIFE OBJECTS   *B-* SHADING A HEAD

Fig. 36.—How Shading Is Done

to make the half-tones, or gradations as it is called, and
when you can do this you are ready to work in colors.

The Materials You Need.[7]—There are several things
you must have to begin the hobby of painting in oils, and
these are (*1*) a canvas or a cardboard, (*2*) the oil colors,
(*3*) some drying oil and turpentine, (*4*) some brushes,
(*5*) a palette, (*6*) a pair of little tin cups, (*7*) a palette
knife, and (*8*) a rest or mahlstick. You should have an
easel to hold the canvas upright, or nearly so, while you
are painting it, and, lastly, a smock to paint in.

[7] All of the materials cited in this chapter are sold by the Devoe and
Raynolds Co., Inc., New York and Chicago. Write to them for their free
illustrated catalogue.

You can buy canvas that is already prepared for painting, and this you can mount on stretchers, that is, wooden frames, or you can buy it already mounted on stretchers. As canvas is quite expensive for practice purposes you can use what is called *Academy Board*, or, cheaper still, you can make a board by taking a sheet of pasteboard— laundry shirt pasteboard will do—and then shellac it and let it dry. The only drawback about using board instead of canvas is that your masterpiece will not last through the ages.

Oil colors come in tubes and you only need half a dozen of these to start with. These colors are (*a*) burnt sienna, (*b*) permanent blue, (*c*) yellow ochre, (*d*) rose madder, (*e*) raw sienna, and (*f*) flake white. You can get the above half-dozen colors in small tubes, called single tubes, for 75 cents, or in large tubes, called double tubes, for $1.30, or very large tubes, called quadruple tubes, for $2.10. You will also need a bottle of purified linseed oil to thin down, that is to reduce the viscosity of the colors, and a bottle of rectified turpentine to clean your brushes with as you use them.

You should have a brush for each color, but you can get along with a sable brush and a couple of bristle brushes. The palette is a thin oval or square board with a thumb-hole in one end and it is on this that you lay the colors you are going to use for the time being. You should have a pair of little tin cups and fix these to the palette and pour a little oil in one and turpentine in the other. The palette knife has a very thin flat blade and it is used to take off any colors you do not want on the canvas. The rest, or mahlstick, is used to rest your hand on when you are painting. If you are working indoors you can get along without an easel but you must have one if you are working outdoors. You can get a folding one made of whitewood for a couple of dollars. A folding stool is also a necessity and a collapsible one will cost you $1.50. Finally, to give you the complex of a real painter you should wear a smock, and, if your money holds out, buy a tam-o'-shanter or a beret, and your equipment will be complete.

How to Paint a Canvas.—Having now your canvas, colors and other materials, you begin by squeezing a little of each color out of the tube on the palette. Put plenty of white on it as this forms the base or body of the mixed colors. The other colors are superimposed on the white base, and this gives it the various tones. To get the different color effects you have only to mix two of the colors together, and to make any color or mixture of colors of a lighter shade or tint mix it with white.

Colors and Color Mixtures

Blue and yellow make green
Blue and red make purple
Blue and white make pale blue
Blue and burnt sienna make black
Raw sienna is a light brown
Burnt sienna is a dark brown

While some painters mix their colors on the palette, it is the better way to put them on the canvas over each other and so get the effect you want. In putting the colors on the canvas stand away a little from it, and you will be able to see the effect you are striving for to better advantage; that is why the brushes are made with long handles.

While turpentine is used to clean the brushes and take off spots, do not use it on the canvas, as it will dissolve the colors. If the colors are very thick, it may take anywhere from *3* days to a week for your painting to dry. You can, however, put a little Japan drier in it, and it will dry in about half the time. When you get through with the day's work, always clean off the brushes with soap, and not with turpentine, as the former preserves them.[8]

Painting with Water Colors.—The technique employed for water color painting is quite different from that of painting with oil colors in that (*1*) in the former you use paper or board to lay your colors on, instead of canvas, and (*2*) the water colors are not mixed as are oil colors, but are laid on one over the other.

How to Begin.—What I have told you about beginning to paint with oil colors, i. e., sketching and shading, is equally applicable to painting with water colors. Now there are four different methods [9] employed for laying on the colors, and to learn all about all of them you should read some book that explains them simply and in detail; you can then choose the one that appeals to you most.

The Material You Use.—To paint with water colors you will need (*1*) some paper, (*2*) a drawing board, (*3*) a

[8] Here are some good books for you to read if you are a beginner in painting in oils: (1) *A Plain Guide to Oil Painting,* by Hume Nesbit, (*$1.00*); *Art of Mixing Things of Color,* by M. E. Prescott, (*$.25*); *The Painter in Oil,* by Daniel Burleigh Parkhurst, (*$2.00*); *How to Mix Colors,* by J. H. Bustanoby, (*$1.00*); and *Landscape Painting,* by F. J. Carlson, (*$5.00*). All of these books are sold by the Devoe and Raynolds Co., New York and Chicago.

[9] These are known as (*1*) the English method, (*2*) the sewing-up method, (*3*) the smooth paper method, and (*4*) the dry brush method.

couple of brushes, (*4*) a box, (*5*) a water bottle, and (*6*) a few other little things. For your trial paintings use the heaviest rough paper in block form and of any size from *5* by *7* to *10* by *18* inches on the edges. Whatman's make a good trial paper as both sides of it can be used. The drawing board should be about *12* by *20* inches on the sides.

You will need only two brushes and these are (*a*) a sign painter's ox-hair lettering brush, that is about ¾ of an inch wide, or a large, flat camel's-hair brush, with which to put on the wash, and (*b*) a medium-size, round, red-sable brush, that comes to a sharp point when it is wet, to put the colors on in line.

You can get water color paints (*a*) in tubes and (*b*) in little porcelain pans. Those in tubes are the best for you to use as they are more economical and easily manipulated. There are many makes and among them are the Newman, Newton, and Deveau. The following colors will be all that you need to start with: (*a*) French ultramarine, (*b*) cobalt violet blue, (*c*) Antwerp blue, (*d*) chrome yellow, (*e*) chrome orange, (*f*) burnt sienna, (*g*) sepia, (*h*) raw umber, (*i*) opaque white, and (*j*) ivory black. The chrome yellows are not permanent colors, and so if you want your paintings to outlast you, then you must use cadmium yellow and orange, but they are more expensive. To the above list you can add a few brilliant coal-tar colors, i. e., turquoise, No. *1;* yellow-green, No. *1;* aureolin, a gold paint, and viridian, a greenish-yellow paint.

You will also need a large japanned metal box, to keep your tubes of paint in and one which has cavities in it for holding the squeezed-out colors. Also a water bottle, to hold the water that is used for melting them up. An ordinary wide-mouth bottle, that will hold about ½ a pint of water, will serve the purpose. Finally, get a piece of cheesecloth, some art gum, a medium-hard pencil, and a low camp stool, when you are ready to sally forth on your painting expedition.

How to Paint with Water Colors.—The first thing to do is to coat the edges of a sheet of paper and paste it to your drawing board. The next thing is to dampen the surface of the paper with a moist sponge, and as it dries it will shrink and be taut. This done, block in the design you are going to paint very lightly with a pencil and then, to take away that papery look, and give the painting a mellow appearance, you must cover the surface of it with a rainbow wash.

To make this mix a little of the various colors with a large amount of water, and then lay the solution on the paper with a to and fro movement of your brush. Finally, paint in the flowers, landscape, or whatever you have in mind for the theme of the picture. If there is any little thing you may want expert advice on just write my friend Mrs. George W. (Emma B. Grieder) Yeatman, 46 Bank Street, New York City, and I am sure she will write and tell you.

Drawing Pastel Pictures.—We borrowed the word pastel from the French, who appropriated it from the Italian *pastello,* and the latter got it from the Latin *pasta* which means *paste.* Pastel crayons are made by grinding purified chalk with pigments of various colors and a binder made either of starch paste or gum tragacanth. Different from oil and water color painting, drawing a pastel picture is quite an easy and simple matter, and it is equally as beautiful as either of them when it is well done.

The Materials You Need.—To draw a pastel picture you will need only two items and these are (*1*) a pastel board, and (*2*) some crayons. The pastel board is made of paper pulp, and it comes in various textures and colors. As a starter get crayons of the following colors: (*a*) a big block of white, (*b*) a sky blue, (*c*) a cobalt blue, (*d*) a chrome yellow, (*e*) a sienna, (*f*) a vermilion, and (*g*) a Mar's red. Schwenke crayons are the best to work with as they are softer than the French crayons, and cheaper as well.

How to Draw the Pictures.—To draw the picture you begin by taking the block of white crayon and rub it all over the rough surface of the pastel board, or wash it as it is called, and then rub it in with your fingers. Now draw a horizon line with your black crayon across the board and shade it off by rubbing your fingers up and down (vertically) over it.

This done, rub in a little blue above it for the clouds and below it for the water. Leave a white spot in the sky for the sun, and put a few white spots in the water for the reflected rays of it. Up to now it won't look much like a picture, but with a couple of graceful strokes of your black crayon for a tree in the foreground, and some dabs with it for the leaves, the whole aspect of it is instantly changed and you will have a pretty pastel with considerable depth to it. My genial friend, George W. Yeatman, the Greenwich Village artist, *46* Bank Street, New York City, initiated me into the gentle mysteries of drawing them, and if there is anything farther that you want to know about the art, write to him and he will give you the desired information.

The Hobby of Modeling.—In the fine arts the word *modeling* is used to mean (*1*) to form a work of art of some plastic material, and (*2*) the act of making a model from which a work of art is to be executed, such as a plaster or a bronze cast, or one that is chiseled out of stone or marble.

Now the desire to model is a mode of expression that is as old as the human race itself and it is inherent in every being of the Genus homo. It usually begins to show itself at a very early age, as is evidenced by the kiddies who make mud-pies and other like objects. Those who have the innate ability to model a face or a form which bears a recognizable resemblance to the thing it is modeled after have the necessary qualifications to become sculptors.

The Things You Need.—There are various outfits for modeling that are made for children, and these can be bought in stationery shops and department stores; they contain the needful things for them to try their little hands at modeling, but if you are to take up the art as a serious hobby you must have the proper appliances and quite a lot of plastic material to work with.[10]

Thus to model a head you will need (*1*) an armature, (*2*) a couple of tools, i. e., a wood tool and a wire tool; and (*3*) several pounds of clay or plasteline. The armature is a support on which the plastic material is mounted so that it can be kept in place while it is being worked.

---

[10] You can get everything you need for modeling of the Devoe and Raynolds Co., Inc., who have a number of stores in New York and Chicago.

You can make a head armature, that is, one on which to model heads, of a stick of wood fixed to a base or, better, of an iron pipe and fittings as shown at *A* in *Fig. 37*. The wood tool is formed of a piece of hardwood about *8* inches long, which is flat on one end, and brought to a point on the other end, as pictured at *B*, while the wire tool has a looped wire with teeth on it on its ends, as

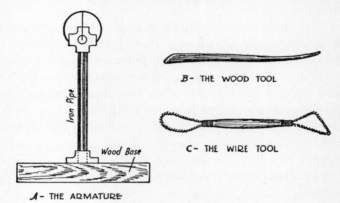

FIG. 37.—THE THINGS YOU NEED FOR MODELING

shown at *C*. It is with these simple tools that you give the final shape to the plastic material you are modeling.

For the modeling material you can use either (*1*) clay or (*2*) plasteline. There are two grades of clay, namely, American clay which costs about *4* or *5* cents a pound, and French clay which costs about *10* cents a pound. To make either kind plastic enough for modeling you have to knead it up with a little water, and then keep wet cloths on it to prevent it from getting too hard while you are using it.

Plasteline is made of clay mixed with oil, and as this keeps it from getting hard you can use it over and over again. There are two grades of it, ordinary plasteline, which costs about *30* cents a pound, and Italian plasteline, which costs about *60* cents a pound; this latter is the kind that is used by professional modelers. It is far cleaner than clay and water to work with, but it is not advisable to use either of them in the drawing room. You can get either of these plastics at any store where artists' materials are sold.

How to Begin.—To model a head the first thing to do is to put a lump of either clay or plasteline on the wire top of the armature and press it in very firmly, or there will be airholes in it, and it will crack or cave in. You should make the head full size, for it is far easier to get the right expression on it than it is on a small one. After you have given it a shape that approximates the form of the head you are going to model, you then put a roughly shaped piece on it for the nose and other pieces for the ears, cheeks, chin and hair.

When you are shaping the features don't try to push the material from one place where it is not needed to another place where it is needed. Instead, cut off the material where there is an excess of it with your wood tool, and put on some where there is a lack of it. This done, take the wire tool and pull the forms together until they meet, then use the flat side of the tool and smooth up the surface.

You can model the eyes as they really are, that is, give them a convex oval form, or hollow out the pupils, which is the easier way, and will make them look far more natural than the former unless you are very talented. In modeling the hair, do not try to put in each separate one, but instead work in masses of it with light and shadow effect, giving an accent to it here and there, the final result of which makes it look like actual hair, as is indicated at *D*.

When you are able to make a fairly well proportioned head you can then try your hand at modeling one which

FIG. 37D.—A MODELED BUST OF LINCOLN

is a likeness of somebody. There are three ways that you can do this, to wit, (*1*) by using a bust that has been made by some other modeler or sculptor, (*2*) from pictures or photographs of a person, and (*3*) from actual life, i. e., a friend who is willing to pose for you.

What I have told you above is but the barest outline of how to begin and to do modeling, but to get all of the practical details you should read *Modeling and Sculpture in the Making,* by C. S. Jaggers.[11]

Should any outstanding question come up you can write to my young friend, Ruth Nickerson, *206* West *82*nd Street, New York City, who is not only a talented modeler, but a very fine sculptor as well, and I am sure she will tell you anything about either of these two arts you may want to know; also about classes, clubs and papers which are devoted to them, as well as the addresses of dealers in modeling materials, stone and marble, art objects for you to make reproductions from, and bronze founders.

The Hobby of Soap and Beeswax Sculpturing.— The difference between (*1*) modeling in clay or plasteline, and (*2*) sculpturing in soap or beeswax is that (*a*) the former, which are plastic materials, are worked into the desired shape with your hands and a couple of simple tools, while (*b*) the latter, which are comparatively hard materials, must be cut to the requisite shape. Further, you can make the object you are working on of any size, while with soap this is confined to the dimensions of the bar of soap.

*The Art of Soap Sculpturing.—*At the *Tenth Annual Soap Sculpturing Competition* nearly *4,000* soap sculptures were entered and exhibited and these represented the efforts of but a fractional part of the soap sculpturing hobbyists that are practising the art at the present time. If you have an artistic temperament and feel impelled to do a statue in stone or marble, here is the way that you can try out your genius without going to the expense that a

[11] Published by the Studio Publications, Inc., *381* Fourth Avenue, N. Y.

studio and its equipment will cost, and the time and labor that such an undertaking would involve.

How to Begin.—The great merit in soap sculpturing lies in the fact that you need only four things and these are (*1*) an artistic eye, (*2*) a bar of Ivory, or other white soap, (*3*) a pocket-knife, and (*4*) a darning needle, or other pointed implement.

The first thing to do is to scrape the bar of soap until the sides of it are perfectly smooth, and then select the object that you are going to make the image of. This done, trace the outline of the object on one side of the bar, as

A- THE TRACED DESIGN   *B*- THE DESIGN CUT OUT   *C*- THE FINISHED SCULPTURE

FIG. 38.—HOW SOAP SCULPTURING IS DONE

shown at *A* in *Fig. 38*, just as you would if you were going to saw it out of a block of wood. Now cut it away until you come to the outline when you will have a flat representation of it, as at *B*.

To give it a realistic appearance you must round off the edges of all parts of it, and give them the forms and dimensions of the model you are working from; finally, put in all of the details, when you will have something or nothing to be proud of, depending on your innate artistic ability and previous training. It should then look like *C*.

Should your *objet d'art* meet with your approbation and you decide you want to keep it, look it over carefully and see if there are any airholes in it. If there are knead a bit of soap in your fingers until it is pliable and then plug them up. Put a drop of water on the plugs and rub them down gently, when the holes will be made invisibly whole.

All that remains to be done now is to finish the surface of it, and this you can do by gently scraping it with the back of your knife; this will act as a kind of a burnisher and produce a nice smooth finish. If you want it to have the appearance of a polish hold it under water and then burnish it with your knife. After it has dried out and aged for some time it will look very like an old ivory carving, and one which you will allow is a very beautiful and intriguing piece of work.

While the best way to learn to sculpture in soap or beeswax is to go ahead and do it, still you will find many helpful suggestions in *A Little Book About Small Sculpture,* by Ernest Bruce Haswell, published by *The National Soap Sculpture Committee, 80* East *11th* Street, New York City, and, I believe, a copy will be sent to you free of charge. Then there is a thirty-one page book called *The Development and Use of Soap Sculpture,* which is also published by the above named Committee. This is a very useful little book and the price of it is *10* cents.

Every year a *Competition for Small Sculptures in White Soap* is held under the auspices of the Committee, the prizes for which are given by the Procter and Gamble people of Cincinnati, Ohio. You can get instruction books and entry blanks by addressing the Committee. At the *10th* Annual Competition nearly *4,000* sculptures were entered, and *28,000* people attended the exhibition, which was held during the month of June, *1934*, at Rockefeller Center, New York City.

The Hobby of Taxidermy.—We get the word *taxi*-dermy (pronounced *tax'*-i-der-mi) from the Greek roots *taxis* which means *to arrange*, and *derma* meaning *skin*, and, it follows, we use it to signify the preparing and mounting of the skins of animals, especially the vertebrates, in a lifelike manner.

The old method of taxidermy consisted of stuffing the skin of the animal with straw, excelsior and clay, but this crude scheme has all but given way to the more recent artistic and scientific practice of making a manikin of fabric and *papier-mâché* of the animal to be preserved and covering this with its tanned skin. From this it is clear that to be a taxidermist of the new school you have to be a modeler or a sculptor of no mean ability, besides possessing genius along several other different lines.

How to Begin.—If you are good at modeling you can start on your career as a taxidermic hobbyist by the simple and costless expedient of catching a mouse, killing it painlessly, measuring it up carefully, and finally skinning it. This done, make a little clay model of it that conforms exactly to the measurements you have taken of it. All you have to do now is to glue or cement the skin to the model, or you can sew the edges of it together under the latter. You can use black-headed pins for the eyes, and if you have done a good job your mouse will look very much as it did in the life.

When you have become quite expert in mounting mice, you can embark on a most unique hobby and that is fashioning very realistic miniature deer and other kinds of big game, by making clay models of them mouse-size, then wetting the skins of the mice and stretching and glueing them on. This clever taxidermic stunt was originated by that past master of hobbies, whose hobby is hobbies, Jeanette Stevens, of *618* West *143rd* Street, New York City.

Having acquired something that approximates proficiency in mounting mice, you can go a step farther and add to your skill by mounting rats, guinea pigs, squirrels and other small animals. Then when some one has a pet cat or a favorite dog whose soul has passed on to its own peculiar celestial abode, the owner will probably be only too glad to have you mount it; in this way, then, you will not only further your technique, but much merit will accrue to you as well, and it won't be long now until you are a full-fledged taxidermist in good standing in your community.

How Trophies Are Mounted.—The processes that are used by the sculptor-taxidermists of the *James L. Clark Studios, Inc.,* *285* Grand Concourse, New York City, for mounting big game specimens are, briefly, as follows: immediately the hunter has killed an animal which he intends to have mounted, he takes accurate measurements and good photographs of it. The skin is then removed from the carcass and either packed in salt or dried in the sun to preserve it. When in due time it reaches the studio the very particular job of preparing it for mounting begins. The first step is to soften it, and this is done by soaking it in water; it is then tanned in a suitable solution and shaved down to the proper thickness.

After it has thus been converted into leather it is treated with oil which makes it permanently *live,* and then rubbed with hardwood sawdust.[12] The tanned skin is then as clean and soft and pliable as when it was on the living animal, and it will never break through or crack up as do those that are mounted *raw,* or which are *pickled* by the older methods.

For the sculptor-taxidermist to mount the skin of the animal so that it be true to life, he must have a working knowledge of animal anatomy, just as a modeler or a sculptor must have in order to make a replica in clay. The first thing he does is to take the measurements of the animal that were made when the hunter killed it, and fashion a clay model just as it was when in the living flesh, so that the muscles, tendons and big veins stand out with vivid realism.

When he has completed it he makes a plaster-of-Paris *piece-mold,* that is a mold formed of a number of separate parts or pieces of it, and from these he builds up a cast, or *manikin* as it is called, of fabric and *papier-mâché,*[13] as pictured in *Fig. 39.* When the manikin is so made it is not more than ¼ of an inch thick, and very light in weight, and it shows all of the finer details of the original model.

The skull of the animal is not used as a framework for the head, but only for taking measurements for the manikin which is in the making. The horns and teeth are fastened to a thin plate of bone, and this is firmly secured to the manikin, while the glass eyes are rigidly set in it. The old-line taxidermists either (1) left the natural cartilages in the ears of the mounted animal and when they dried out

[12] In the James L. Clark Studios, Inc., New York City, the skins are tumbled in revolving drums that are partially filled with hardwood sawdust.

[13] While builder's paper can be used for making the manikin, it will lack detail and bend and warp out of shape.

they crumpled up, or (2) used flimsy paper forms in their stead.

The sculptor-taxidermist does not discard the cartilages of the natural ears of the animal he is mounting until he

Fig. 39.—Mr. Clark Modeling a Roosevelt Hartebeeste for the National Museum

has made exact duplicates of them in sheet metal. This method gives the mounted animal an individual character that makes it a personal trophy, instead of just a nondescript figure. Finally, the tanned skin is put on the manikin and fixed to it for all time with a special cement.

If you are interested in mounting game specimens, tanning furs and making leather, I would suggest that you write to the Secretary of the *Northwestern School of Taxidermy,* Omaha, Nebraska. This is a correspondence school and it teaches taxidermy at home by mail. I don't know just what the tuition is for the course of lessons, but it is not, I imagine, very much.

CHAPTER VIII

THE PHOTOGRAPHIC ARTS HOBBIES

The Photographic Hobbies.—We get the word *photography* (pronounced fo-*tog'*-ra-fe) from the Greek roots *photos* which means *light,* and *graphos* meaning *to write;* as its name indicates, it is the art of producing images by the action of light, or other form of radiant energy, on a sensitive surface, such as a dry plate or a film.

It was George Eastman of Rochester, New York, who invented the hobby of photography, and this he did by making it possible for every one and his brother to make pictures. I shall not, therefore, go into the universal hobby of making ordinary snapshots, but, instead, tell you about some that are a little out of the beaten track, and these I have divided into four groups, namely, (*1*) trick photography, (*2*) novel photography, (*3*) scientific photography, and (*4*) moving-picture photography.

The Hobby of Trick Photography.—*Trick photography* is the making of false and fantastic images so that the observer can't tell where the truth ends and the lie begins, or the other way about. It gives a double-barreled kick that you can't get out of any kind of legitimate photography. Now the trick photographic hobbies I shall tell you about are (*1*) firelight and moonlight effects, (*2*) the lying camera, (*3*) caricature photography, (*4*) insect photography, and (*5*) spirit photography.

168

Firelight and Moonlight Effects.—You can make some very pretty and striking photographs by simulating these effects, and you can do it anywhere without the aid of a fireplace or the pale, cold moon. The *firelight effect* is produced by building up an imitation fireplace and then developing the print in a bath of *firelight-red*. The *moonlight* effect is produced by putting a print of a landscape, or other scene, in a bath of *moonlight blue*. Panchromatic plates or films plus suitable filters should be used, and you will find the formulas and procedure for producing these effects in my *Amateur Photographer's Handbook*.[1]

The Lying Camera.—The camera is held up as a shining example of truth in its nudist form, for nothing escapes the power of its magic eye, and every detail, however minute, is recorded by it on a sensitive film. It is, however, in the matter of relative proportion that the camera handles the truth so carelessly.

As an example, when you make a *close-up* of a person in a reclining position, with his feet nearest the camera and his head in an axial line with them and the lens, the result will be a picture which shows them (his feet) to be of elephantine size and his head of peanut size.

Another lying photograph is the fisherman's delight, for every fisherman is a potential liar or else he wouldn't be a fisherman. In this kind of a trick photograph, the fisherman holds a small fish (which he probably has bought) in front of the camera, and he stands back of it in an axial line with it and the lens, as shown at *A* in *Fig. 40*. Now when you get a print of the negative you will find the fish is almost as big as the fisherman, as at *B*.

Grotesque Insect Photography.—It has long been

[1] Published by the Thomas Y. Crowell Company, New York.

known that man is an insect in a woman's estimation, but that insects are dimunitive men was left for the genius of my friend, Dr. Lehman Wendell, to discover, and he certainly has the photographic proof of it down to a fine point.

To make the photographs, you must catch your insect, such as a grasshopper, or a cricket, and kill it with chloroform; then use a sheet of white or black paper for

A - HOW IT IS DONE   *B*- HOW IT LOOKS WHEN DONE

Fig. 40.—An Easy Way to Catch a Big Fish

a background and build a miniature foreground up of moss, twigs, and the like. The accessories are also taken from Nature's storehouse; thus if you want a canoe you use a pea-pod, if a telescope make one of straw, etc. Having prepared the scene, you pose the insect for his picture and, if needs be, prop him up with bits of wire. Finally photograph him using a double extension bellows camera, or a supplementary lens, and there you have him in the rôle of a human being as pictured in *Fig. 41*. You will find a very good article on *Insect Photography* in *The Miniature Camera, 1933*.

Caricature Photography.—We get the word *caricature* from the Italian verb *caricatura* which means *to exaggerate,* and a *caricature photograph* is a portrait of a person in which the body is so minimized in relation to his head that he looks quite ridiculous and often positively funny.

The way that photographs of this kind are generally made is to use a *comic foreground* and this consists of

FIG. 41.—MAKING GROTESQUE INSECT PHOTOGRAPHS

a sheet of heavy cardboard on which is painted the dwarfed body of a man riding, not a hobby, but in a road lizard. The sitter holds the foreground up to and under his chin and when you have made a print of the negative it will look like *Fig. 42.* You can get some remarkable effects in projection printing by bending the paper out of the focal plane after you have stopped down the lens.

Making Spirit Photographs.—This is a wild and woolly hobby that you can ride into the shadowy beyond with mystery hanging onto its tail, the end-product of which will give a thrill to those who have a flare for the uncanny. Now there are two kinds of spirit photographs, to wit, those that are made (*1*) innocently and with no intent to deceive, and (*2*) accidentally on purpose with malice aforethought and every intention to deceive.

These latter are the kind that we are interested in here and now. There are several ways by which you can make alleged spirit photographs, and one of them is to use a

Fig. 42.—How Caricatures Are Made

pinhole camera, that is one in which a pinhole takes the place of the usual lens. The first thing to do is to make an exposure on a plate, or film, of the head of the person who is to pose as the spirit; you then take the disk of brass that has the pinhole in it, out of the camera and put the regular lens in the latter in its place; this done you make another exposure on the same plate, or film, of another subject who is to represent the real flesh and blood being.

Now when you develop and fix the plate, or film, in the usual way and make a print of it, there will be two images on it, the first of which will be dim, unquestionably a spirit, and hazy, thin as air and apparently transparent, while the latter will be a strong, healthy-looking individual who is at once recognizable as being a member of the living world, and there you have your spirit photograph, as pictured in *Fig. 43*.

FIG. 43.—A SPIRIT (?) PHOTOGRAPH

Novel Photographic Hobbies.—Instead of frittering your time away on trick photographic hobbies, out of which nothing more will accrue to you than a lot of mischievous fun, I would suggest that you take up some one of the more serious branches of the art, of which there are many. In the last analysis, however, you must let your conscience be your guide.

Now there are several outstanding branches of photography that you can take up, any one of which will provide a hobby for you of the most absorbing kind, and one that you can eat and sleep with. While all of the various branches are not new, they are so fascinating it does not matter which one you choose, you can't go wrong. The four novel branches of photography I shall tell you about are (*1*) miniature camera photography, (*2*) stereophotography, (*3*) telephotography and (*4*) color photography.

The Hobby of Miniature Camera Photography.— Miniature camera photography consists simply of making very small negatives, i. e., ½ by ¾ of an inch on the edges, which is half the size of the standard moving picture frame, as a single shot is called, to *1* by *1*½ inches on the edges, which is twice the size of a standard frame, and then enlarging them.

In the early days of dry plate photography, cameras for the hobbyist were usually *5* by *7* or *8* by *10* and this was a heavy, bellows affair, that weighed enough over plenty. From the time George Eastman adapted the film to amateur work in *1889*, the size and weight of cameras were steadily reduced. The *miniature camera,* or *minican,* as it is sometimes called, made its first appearance in Germany in *1924* and it then found its way to the United States, where it has become extremely popular.

Today the tendency is to get away from the larger cameras and to use the minican for all purposes. An enlarged print is then made of the miniature negative; since these little cameras are fitted with high speed and high power lenses, it is perfectly feasible to enlarge a miniature negative *10* to *15* times without any appreciable loss of detail. The reduction in the size of the cameras has

been largely made possible by the invention of new and
finer grained emulsions with which the films are coated.

Carl Zeiss, Inc.,[2] make a miniature camera called the
Contax and this has *12* separate and distinct interchange-
able lenses, including several for telephoto work, and *10*

FIG. 44.—THE ZEISS NEW AUTOMATIC MINIATURE CAMERA

The Ikron Super-Nettel takes pictures on standard 35 mm. motion-
picture film size of picture, 24 by 35 mm; focal plane shutter with
speeds from ⅕ to ¹⁄₁₀₀₀ second; fitted with F 3.5 or F 2.5 Tessar lens.

shutter speeds, making it the most versatile miniature
hobby camera now on the market. The Zeiss *New Automatic* miniature camera is shown in *Fig. 44.* E. Leitz,

[2] Carl Zeiss, Inc., are located at *485* Fifth Avenue, New York City,
E. Leitz, Inc., at *60* East *10*th Street, New York City. Bausch and Lomb,
at Rochester, New York. You will find other firms listed in *The Miniature Camera,* a magazine published at *23* Lexington Avenue, Suite *305,*
New York City.

Inc., Bausch and Lomb, Eastman, and several other optical companies also make miniature cameras and accessories, and you should get in touch with them.

So great is the interest in miniature camera photography that *The Miniature Camera Club,* of New York,
has been incorporated, and under its auspices a magazine
called *The Miniature Camera* is published monthly. If
you want to take up miniature camera photography either
as a pictorial or a technical hobby, your one best bet
is to subscribe for the magazine, join the club if possible, and get in touch with the various manufacturers
of miniature cameras.

The Hobby of Stereophotography.—In the olden,
golden days before the motor car, radio and moving pictures were invented, *stereophotography,* that is, *stereo-
scopic photography,* was one of the great hobbies, and
very wonderful it was and, for that matter, still is. Now
stereophotography is the art of making and showing photographs in such a way that they appear to stand out
in relief exactly as though you were looking at the real
object or landscape.

Since all material things in nature have three dimensions, i. e., length, breadth and depth, and a photographic
print, as far as the eye is concerned, has only two dimensions, to wit, length and breadth, it follows that the picture in which the third dimension is missing lacks the
effect that depth gives, namely, the perspective and soli-
darity of the original object or view.

To produce the wonderful result of making two dimensions look like three dimensions you must make two negatives of the object or landscape which are slightly separated to correspond to the distance your eyes are apart.

Now when you look at the two pictures, which are made from the negatives, through a simple optical instrument called a *stereoscope,* each eye sees only one of the pictures but the images of them on their respective retinas are carried by the optic nerve to the brain where they are registered exactly one on the other, and it is this that gives you the sensation of depth and distance.

A further amazing thing that a stereographic camera does is to correct the results of so-called distorted perspective. Thus when you make a picture with a single lens of a high building with a tilted camera in order to get it all on the plate or film, it (the building) will appear to be leaning over backward. Again, if you make a picture with a single lens of a person with his feet nearest the camera and his head in alignment with them and the lens, his feet will look disproportionally large.

If, however, you make a picture of either the building or the person under like conditions with a stereo-camera the distorted perspective disappears, when, it follows, the picture will look absolutely normal. You can get a stereo-camera in various styles and sizes and at different prices.[3] (The Eastman Company of Rochester, New York, make a regulation one that they called the *Stereo-Kodak* and another that is known as the *Stereo-Auto-Graflex.*)

E. Leitz, Inc., make a *stereo-attachment* which can be used for taking stereo-pictures with their different miniature camera models. The attachment is fitted over the single lens of your camera and the light is split up into two parts by means of a series of prisms. To view the usual stereo-pictures made with a pair of lenses, you must

[3] Write to Burleigh Brooks, *127* West *42*nd St., N. Y. for a description of his *Heidoscope.*

have a *stereoscope* and this you can get for a dollar or less; to view the pictures made with a stereo-attachment and a single lens you must have a *stereo-viewer* and this will cost you in the neighborhood of *$40.00*.

The Hobby of Telephotography.—Telephotography is the art and practice of taking pictures of objects at a distance so that an enlarged image of them is had. This is done by means of a *telephotographic lens*, or *telephoto-lens* as it is called for short, which gives an enlarged image on the plate or film just as a telescope gives an enlarged image on the retina of the eye.

If you had a camera with a very long bellows extension, you could make telephoto pictures with an ordinary view lens, but as this is not practical an ordinary short extension camera is used and the telephoto lens is made with a long focus which amounts to the same thing. A telephoto lens is not only useful in taking pictures of distant objects as a whole, but it is especially adapted for taking small parts and details of buildings, and the like, that are too high to get with an ordinary view lens. You can also use it for portrait work to get better perspective.

In commercial *aërophotography,* that is photography from an airplane, the camera is usually a long extension one and an ordinary anastigmat [4] lens is used with it. For the purpose of the hobbyist who is doing a lot of flying, an ordinary short extension camera with a telephoto lens is the most suitable equipment. If you are a miniature camera hobbyist you can put a telephoto lens on it and get some wonderful long distance pictures.

The Hobby of Natural Color Photography.—What we call *natural color photography* is the process of making

[4] This is a lens that is free from *astigmatism.*

photographs of an object or landscape in their natural colors. Now the making of natural color photographs is infinitely harder than making black and white photographs because in the latter the chemical change set up in the silver salts is due to the light that acts on them, while in the former there is no simple way known at the present time for producing the various colors by chemical action. It is, however, possible to make color photographs on both glass (transparencies and lantern slides) and paper (paper prints) by a more or less mechanical arrangement of the necessary colors.[5]

Briefly, the above process consists of making three exposures, the first one through a red glass screen, the second through a green glass screen, and the third through a blue-violet glass screen, as these are the three *optical* primary colors of nature. A positive transparency is then made from each negative, and when these are viewed through like color screens and the images are superimposed one on the other, the resultant picture will stand out in the natural colors of the object or view.

At the present time there are several modifications of the above process on the market and among these are (*1*) *the trichrome carbro printing process,* (*2*) the *natural color print film* (Belcolor proof sheets), (*3*) the *Agfa-Leica natural color process,* and (*4*) the *Lumière Filmcolor.* To make natural color transparencies by any of the above processes is an easy matter and they are beautiful beyond description; to make natural color paper prints is something else again, and to produce acceptable ones requires technical skill of a high order.

[5] These processes are described in detail in my *Amateur Photographers' Handbook,* published by the Thomas Y. Crowell Company, N. Y.

There are several good books on natural color photography, and a card to *George Murphy, Inc., 57* East *9*th Street, New York City, will bring you the names and prices of them, and also full instructions for making natural color photographs by the trichrome carbro process, and the natural color print film system, while a card to *E. Leitz, Inc., 60* East *10*th Street, New York City, will bring you directions for Agfa color photography for the Leica cameras, and, finally for the Lumière Filmcolor write to *R. J. Fitzsimmons, 75* Fifth Avenue, New York City.

Scientific Photographic Hobbies.—There are a hundred ways, more or less, in which photography is used to aid and abet the various branches of science, and any one of which will provide you with a hobby that you can ride to the end of your days. And let me say right here that a hobby of this kind will invigorate your soul and at the same time add mightily to your store of knowledge. The four chief photographic hobbies are (*1*) astrophotography, (*2*) microphotography, (*3*) X-ray photography, and (*4*) strobophotography.

The Astrophotographic Hobby.—Astrophotography is the art of photographing the stars and other heavenly bodies. If you point an ordinary camera toward the northern heavens on a clear and moonless night so that the lens and the North Star are in alignment with each other, and then let the shutter remain open for several hours you will get a photographic record of the apparent diurnal motion of those stars that are within a few degrees of the north celestial pole as shown in *Fig. 45*.

To make a photograph of the stars and other heavenly bodies so that a sharp image of them is formed on the plate or film, you do not need a camera but simply a plate holder that is secured to the eye-end of the telescope. Moreover, this latter must be an equatorial, clock-driven one, that is one which is so mounted that the axes of

FIG. 45.—PHOTOGRAPHIC RECORD OF THE APPARENT DIURNAL MOTIONS OF STARS WITHIN A FEW DEGREES OF THE NORTH CELESTIAL POLE. EXPOSURE, 4 HOURS, 10 MINUTES.

motion are at right angles to each other. When a telescope of this kind is driven by clockwork, it moves at exactly the same speed as that at which the earth revolves on its axis and this keeps the heavenly body stationary in the field of view.

To make *astrophotographs,* as photographs made with

a telescope are called, you must focus the latter on the heavenly body you want to take and then open the shutter. To keep the image on the plate or film as sharp as possible, you must look through the finder of the telescope every little while and adjust the latter with your hands. This is necessary, for while a clock-driven telescope is accurate enough for making visual observations of a heavenly body, it is not sufficiently accurate for taking astrophotographs.

The Hobby of Making Photomicrographs.—A photomicrograph is an enlarged photograph of a microscopic object taken with a camera that is attached to the eye-end of a microscope. J. B. Reade, of England, was the first hobbyist who took up the art of making photomicrographs; this he did nearly *100* years ago, when he made a photograph of a magnified image of a flea by attaching a camera to his microscope. Now there are two ways to make photomicrographs and these are (*1*) with an ordinary camera, and (*2*) with a camera fixed to a microscope.

With an Ordinary Camera.—You do not need a microscope to make low-power photomicrographs, i. e., where the enlarged image is between *4* and *10* diameters of the object. What you must have, however, is a camera that has an extension bellows, and then use a lens of short focus in it when it acts as a kind of enlarging lantern. In this case the object to be photographed corresponds to the picture on the lantern slide and the plate or film to the screen on which the slide is projected.

With a Microscope.—To make photographs of highly enlarged images of objects you must fix a camera to your microscope as pictured in *Fig. 46.* A photomicroscope consists of a microscope which is mounted on a heavy base to which is secured a standard that rigidly supports the camera. The latter can be turned out of the way when you want to visually examine the object.

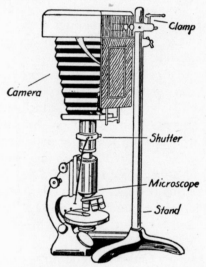

FIG. 46.—How Photomicrographs Are Made

Three things are necessary to make sharp and clear photomicrographs, and these are (*1*) a good light, (*2*) to have your microscope and camera absolutely free from vibration, and (*3*) to have the image of the object focussed as sharply as possible. If you are interested in taking up photomicrography as a hobby write to Carl Zeiss, Inc., E. Leitz, Inc., and the Bausch and Lomb Company.

The Hobby of X-Ray Photography.—What we call

X-rays are waves in the ether each of which is *1,000* times shorter than the shortest wave length of light.[6] As you probably know, X-rays will pass through opaque substances such as paper, wood, flesh, and other substances whose densities are small.

The apparatus that is needed to set up X-rays is (*a*) an X-ray tube and (*b*) a source of high-voltage alternating current, such as an electric machine, an induction coil,

FIG. 47.—How to See the Bones in Your Hand

or a transformer. The X-ray tube, in its simplest form, consists of a bulb-shaped tube in which there is sealed a concave metal cathode, and a flat surface metal anode which is set at an angle of *45* degrees to the cathode; the tube is then exhausted to about one-millionth of an atmosphere. The way an X-ray tube is connected up to an induction coil and this to a battery is shown in *Fig. 47.*

[6] This is about $\frac{165}{10,000,000}$ths of an inch.

There are two ways by which you can see the effects of the X-rays, and these are (*1*) by making a photograph of the shadow of an object cast by the rays on a plate or film, and (*2*) by looking at the shadow of an object cast by them on a fluorescent screen. To make an X-ray photograph or *radiograph* as it is called, of your own, or some one else's hand, or of an object of any kind, you need only to put a dry plate or a film in a plate holder, or a light-proof envelop, in your dark-room just as though you were going to take a picture with your camera. This done lay it on the table and place the object you are going to make a radiograph of on top of it. Now adjust the tube so that it will be about *10* inches above and directly over the plate holder. Finally, turn on the current and the tube will be energized and give off X-rays.

After you have made the exposure, develop, fix and dry the dry plate or film in the usual way when you will have an X-ray, or radiograph, negative of the object, and you can then make a print of it.

To *see* the bones in your hand, coins in a purse, or other small hidden objects, or rather the shadows of them, you must use a *fluoroscope*.[7] This consists of a pyramidal shaped box on the small end of which is fitted a hood to keep the outside light from reaching the eyes, and to the larger end of which is fixed a fluorescent screen. This latter is made of a sheet of cardboard covered with a layer of crystals of calcium tungstate or with barium platino-cyanide.

By placing your hand against the fluorescent screen and looking through the other end of it, and then adjust-

---

[7] We get the word *fluoroscope* from the Greek roots *fluor* which means *to flow*, and *skopos* meaning *to view*.

ing the X-ray tube so that the rays will be thrown on the latter, you can clearly see a shadow-picture of the bones in your hand. This curious result is due to the screen becoming fluorescent under the action of the X-rays, as they easily pass through the fleshy parts of your hand, while the bones stop them, and so a shadow of them is cast on the screen.

If you want to take up *radiography,* as X-ray work is called, as a hobby, write to the Central Scientific Company, *460* East Ohio Street, Chicago, Illinois, for information concerning the outfit you need.

The Hobby of Making Stroboscopic Photographs.— This is one of the most unique hobbies of all those that come under the head of science, while the extraordinary effects you can get with it is a never-ending source of wonder and, it follows, of mystical pleasure. Now we get the word *stroboscope* from the Greek roots *strobos* which means *whirling* and *skopos* meaning *to view;* in other words it means *to see* that which is whirling, but it has a much broader meaning than this, to wit, to see an object which is moving very rapidly, as though it were standing still.

A stroboscope is an apparatus for seeing and photographing the various phases of a rotary, or reciprocating, motion by means of a periodically interrupted light, and in its simplest form it consists of a cardboard disk, about a foot in diameter, on which there is one or more marks. The disk is fixed on the end of a spindle and this is mounted on a pair of standards so that it can be rapidly revolved.

If, now, you turn the disk fast enough, the lines on it will appear to the eye to run together, and you will see them as a few concentric streaks. Now set an induction coil close to the front of the disk, and then energize it by turning on the current when sparks will be set up between the electrodes. This done, darken the room and rotate the disk, when as each spark appears the disk is lighted up and you will see the lines on it just as though it (the disk) were standing still. The reason it appears as if it were stationary is because the speed of the disk is relatively slow compared with the length of time the spark lasts.

Stroboscopic outfits are made by both the *General Electric Company*, of Schenectady, New York, and the *Westinghouse Electric and Machine Company*, of East Pittsburgh, Pennsylvania. An outfit consists of (*1*) either a neon tube or a mercury vapor lamp, (*2*) a power pack, (*3*) a contactor, and (*4*) either a synchronous motor or an oscillation unit. Lack of space will not permit me to go into detail concerning the way these parts are made and work but you will find them fully described in my book, *The New World of Science*.[8]

It will suffice to say here, then, that either the tube or the lamp will set up *100,000* or more flashes per second. To make a rotating disk appear to be standing still you must connect the contactor with the shaft of the motor which drives it. The contactor has a make and break device fixed to it and this makes the tube or lamp flash every time the disk completes a revolution.

In the same way you can make any device that has a rotating, or a small reciprocating motion, such as a wheel, a poppet valve, a valve spring or a violin string, seem to be frozen in their movements, when it is easy to photograph them.

[8] Published by the J. B. Lippincott Company, Philadelphia.

Where it is not possible to synchronize the flashes with the moving object by means of the contactor, as, for example, drops of water that form a stream which flows from a tap, an oscillation unit is used, and with this you can make the tube or lamp flash as many times per second as you want it to. By accurately timing the flashes

Fig. 48.—Falling Water Photographed by the Synchronized Light of a Stroboscope Apparatus

of light to the frequency with which the drops of water fall you can make them seem to be suspended in the air as shown in *Fig. 48*. Or they can be made to fall very slowly, or, still more mystifying, to ascend from the surface on which they fall and go back into the tap, just as a moving picture film when it is run backward through the projector will reverse the direction of the object or subject which is being thrown on the screen.

The Moving Picture Hobby.—Taking and projecting moving pictures at home is a comparatively recent hobby, but once that you get a taste of the throbs and thrills of being a cameraman, an operator, a screen star, a director, and a producer all rolled into one, you will be *100* per cent for it to the end of your born days.

Now different from the many hobbies that you can take up in which you isolate yourself and get the pleasure and enjoyment out of it all by your lonesome, taking and projecting moving pictures will make every member of your family a co-hobbyist with you. The scenario has never been written that can begin to interest and entertain you and yours like the drama of real life in which each member of your family makes his entrance, plays his little part, and then makes his exeunt, i. e., retires from the scene.

To see yourself and those who are closest to you on the silver screen at the various stages of life's journey is a biographical record that you will enjoy throughout the years to come, and it will bring back happy memories when all else has vanished into the dim past. "Looka! what's this? The million-dollar smile of Betsy, and the smile-that-won't-come-off of Bobby! And to think they are both married and have kiddies of their own! It seems but yesterday when I shot them!" And the wonderful part of it all is that you can turn back the hands of time and see them as they were whenever you want to and as often as you have the urge to do so.

The Movie Camera and Projector.—To make home moving pictures your hobby, you must have (*1*) a movie camera, and (*2*) a movie projector. A movie camera, which is pictured at *A* in *Fig. 49,* is made just like an ordinary camera in that it has a lens, a shutter and carries a roll of film, but different from it, it has a rotating shutter, and this is geared to the mechanism that feeds the film past the lens.

The shutter has a sector cut out of it, so that when the film stops back of the lens, the opening lets the light from the latter pass through it and so makes the exposure. The film has perforations along its edges, and it is pulled along back of the lens as it is called, one frame at a time. The cam and claw of the camera is operated by a mechanism that consists of gears and levers which are worked by either turning a crank-handle or a coiled spring. The shutter mechanism is so made that from *8* to *32* frames, or pictures, are exposed per second, which is the number that must be thrown on the screen by the projector to give the effect of continuous motion when you are looking at it.

The movie projector, see *B,* is made like a magic lantern in that it has a projecting lens, a condensing lens and a source of light; in addition to these elements it also has a rotary shutter and a cam and claw mechanism for starting the film, pulling it through and stopping it. Like the camera, the shutter mechanism is so made that from *8* to *32* frames, or pictures, can be projected on the screen each second. This, then, is briefly how the camera and projector are made and work.

Kinds of Movie Cameras.—There are several different makes of movie cameras on the market, and these are listed at various prices. The cheapest one I know of is the Keystone Model C,[9] and it costs *$12.50.* It has a monocular view finder with which you can see quickly

---

[9] This is made by the Keystone Mfg. Co., *288* A St., Boston, Mass.

and accurately the desired action or scene exactly as you want it on the screen. The mechanism is operated by turning a crank, and a finger-type movement feeds the film with hairline accuracy. This camera takes an amateur standard *16*-millimeter film, and you can use either

A- SHOOTING A SCENE   *B-* PROJECTING THE PICTURE

FIG. 49.—THE MOVING PICTURE HOBBY

a *50-* or a *100*-foot reel in it; further, you can load it in daylight just as you do an ordinary camera.

The *Keystone Company* also make a couple of other cameras and both of these are known as Model A, the only difference in them being in the lenses they are fitted with and, it follows, this makes a difference in the price of them. The cheaper model has an *f 3.5* lens, and this costs *$35.00*, while the most costly one has an *f 1.5* lens [10] and this costs *$72.00*.

[10] The speed of the lens is indicated by the letter and number. The *f* system is fully explained in my *Amateur Photographer's Handbook,* published by the Thomas Y. Crowell Co., New York.

The *Eastman Kodak Company,* Rochester, New York, make a very fine movie camera called the Cine-Kodak Special. It is intended for serious workers who want to go beyond the average amateur movie-making technique. It is also a good camera for doctors, physicists, biologists, engineers, teachers, etc. For a detailed description and price of it write to the above named company.

Kinds of Movie Projectors.—Curiously enough you can get a cheap movie projector for less money than you can get a cheap movie camera. Thus a Keystone Junior Model E-*65* projector can be had for as little as *$5.00.* It has a reel capacity of *100* feet and projects a picture *20* by *26* inches at a distance of *10* feet, it is driven by a hand crank, and you can get the same projector equipped with a motor drive for *$15.00.*

Another and better projector is the Model D-*62,* and its list price is *$27.50.* It has a reel capacity of *400* feet and a *6*-volt *64*-candle-power lamp. It is fitted with a motor drive and a speed regulator, and projects a picture *40* by *52* inches at a distance of *24* feet. The Model A-*75* projector sells for *$55.00.* It also has a reel capacity of *400* feet and is equipped with a *300*-watt lamp. It is also motor driven and has a speed regulator.

The Model A-*78* approximates a theater quality projector and you can buy one for *$79.50.* It shows sharp and flickerless movies. It has a reel capacity of *400* feet, uses a *500*-watt lamp and makes a picture up to *14* feet wide at a distance of *75* feet. It is operated by a heavy duty *110*-volt motor and has a high speed rewind gear and a cooling system.

A very fine projector is the Eastman Kodascope which is made in two models, i. e., the K-*50,* which has a reel capacity of *400* feet and is equipped with a *500*-watt lamp. It is listed at *$199.50*—and so you might as well call it *$200.00* and be done with it. The K-*75* likewise has a reel capacity of *400* feet and is fitted with a *750* watt lamp. It sells for *$230.00*. For a detailed description of these projectors write to the Eastman Company.

About the Films You Use.—All of the above cameras and projectors are made to use amateur standard *16*-millimeter (mm) film, i. e., one that is ⅝ of an inch wide, whereas the professional standard film is *35* mm. wide (*1*⅜ inches). Since the amateur film is not so wide as the professional film, the frames or pictures are proportionately less in height, so that it takes as long to project *400* feet of film of the former as it does to project *1,000* feet of the latter.

The *Eastman Company* make three kinds of amateur movie films, (*1*) the panchromatic film, (*2*) the super-sensitive panchromatic film, and (*3*) the super-sensitive kodacolor film. The first named pan film is sensitive to the color range of light; the super-sensitive pan film is sensitive to all of the colors of light, and is especially quick to register red and orange light. It is twice as fast as the regular pan film and about *3* times as fast with artificial light when incandescent lamps are used than the latter is. The kodacolor film reproduces scenes and subjects just as you see them with the full range of natural colors.

About Negative and Positive Films.—When you have shot the scene or subject, that is, exposed the film, it is then developed and fixed in the usual way, and you have a negative, just as you do in making ordinary snapshots. Now in order to project the pictures, you must make a positive from or of the negative, and this you can do in two ways, namely by (*1*) contact printing, and (*2*) reversing the negative.

The former is the way that all ordinary positives are made, and where more than one of them is wanted, this is the only way. But where only one positive is needed as for home projection, it is much cheaper and less troublesome to change the negative into a positive. There are several ways that this can be done, but the one that is recommended by the makers of the film is based on re-exposure and development after it has been immersed in a reversing bath. For a detailed description of making a positive from a negative, write to the Eastman Company who will send it to you free of charge.

However, just as about *90* per cent of those who take snapshots with a hand camera have their films developed and prints made by professional processers, so you can have your movie films developed and made into positives at a processing station. The Eastman Company has a large number of them scattered throughout the United States and by writing to it you can find the one that is nearest to you. The first cost of the film also includes the development of it and converting it into a positive when it is ready to run through your projector.

CHAPTER IX

ABOUT MUSICAL HOBBIES

IF you want a hobby that is bridled and saddled and ready to ride at a moment's notice, one that will sooth your savage breast when it is weary, and elevate your soul half-way to heaven when all is going well with you, then get a musical instrument and learn to play it.

Now, as you know, there are numerous kinds of musical instruments, and if you are at all melodiously inclined, you can take up any one of them that your esthetic nature fancies, and play, or learn to play it, without the slightest pain—that is to yourself. I have, however, written this chapter for the benefit of the hobbyist who would fain play an instrument and who is strictly in the beginner's class.

The Jew's-Harp Hobby.—The *jew's-harp*, or *jew's-trump* as it is occasionally called, is preëminently the hobby of the small boy, and it belongs in the same category as the peg-top, the jack-knife and the fishing pole. To get the best music out of it you have to be about *10* years old, go barefoot, look like Huck Finn, and trudge down the hot, dusty road that leads to the old swimmin' hole.

The jew's-harp is a small lyre-shaped musical instrument that has a thin, metal tongue, one end of which is fastened to the base of the frame while the other and free end is bent over. To play the harp, you must hold it between your teeth and then strike the free end of the tongue rhythmically with your finger, as shown in *Fig. 50,* when it will vibrate and give forth sounds as mournful as ever a Jew made at the wailing wall of Jerusalem. To make it produce different tones you need only to change the size and shape of the cavity of your mouth

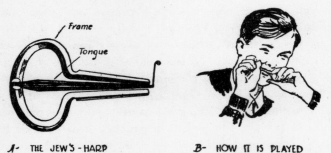

A- THE JEW'S - HARP   B- HOW IT IS PLAYED

FIG. 50.—THE JEW'S-HARP AND HOW IT IS PLAYED

which reinforces the various harmonics of the fundamental tone.

The Ocarina, or Sweet Potato Hobby.—The *ocarina* (pronounced ok-a-*re'*-na), or, as it is popularly called, the *sweet potato,* because it looks like an elongated potato, gets its name from the Italian *oca* which means *goose,* and *rina* meaning *little,* for the very good reason that it is shaped like the body of a diminutive goose as pictured at *A* in *Fig. 51.* It is a simple toy wind instrument that is made of terra-cotta with a projecting mouthpiece and has *8* holes. When you play it, it gives forth soft, sweet, whistling tones quite like those of a flute.

The holes in the ocarina are lettered and numbered

so that you can see just what they are, and to play it, you close up all the holes with your fingers; to produce the different tones you blow into it and raise the finger that is on the hole which gives the tone you want. This little instrument costs from *25* cents for one in the soprano key of *C,* to *$1.00* for one in the bass key of *C.*

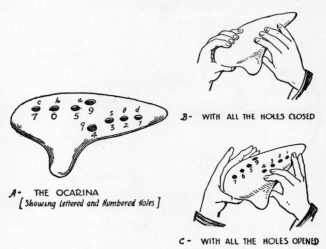

B- WITH ALL THE HOLES CLOSED

A- THE OCARINA
[*Showing Lettered and Numbered Holes*]

C - WITH ALL THE HOLES OPENED

FIG. 51.—THE OCARINA AND HOW IT IS PLAYED

Or if you want to form an *ocarina quartet* you can get four of them that are tuned to harmonize with each other for *$2.50.*

You do not need to know anything about music, or do any studying, to play the ocarina, for an instruction sheet goes with each one, that shows in pictures just how to finger it, as shown at *A* and *C.*

The Harmonica Hobby.—While the *harmonica,* which is its proper name, or *harmonicon,* as the highbrows term it, or just *mouth-organ,* as nine-tenths of those who play it call it, is a real musical instrument, it is chiefly a boys' hobby, though there are many men who play it and like it, but these are only boys who have never grown up.

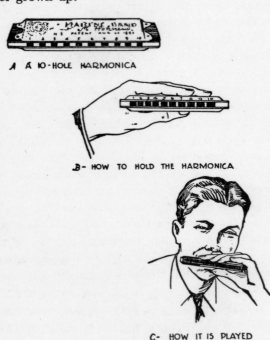

A   A 10-HOLE HARMONICA

B- HOW TO HOLD THE HARMONICA

C- HOW IT IS PLAYED

FIG. 52.—THE HARMONICA AND HOW IT IS PLAYED

The harmonica is a small wind instrument, see *Fig. 52,* that contains two sets of tuned metal reeds, one end of each one of which is fixed to the frame so that the other end can freely vibrate. To play it you hold it between your lips and then blow (exhale) into the holes of it when the air that goes through it makes one set of the reeds vibrate, and when you draw the air in through it (inhale), it makes the other set of reeds vibrate.

Kinds of Harmonicas.—M. Hohner, Inc., of New York City, is the chief harmonica maker in this country, and the company makes many different models. The cheapest of them has *20* reeds, and the most costly has *192* reeds. They range in price from *$.35* to *$2.50,* and you can buy them at any music store.

If you are a beginner, the first thing you should do before you buy a harmonica is to get a booklet written by G. Valentine, Director of Music, Newtown High School, New York City, called *The Art of Playing the Harmonica,* and published by H. Hohner, Inc. This will give you a description of the various instruments, the note range of them, and a number of musical selections which involve two, three, and four, part harmony work.[1]

Learning to Play the Harmonica.—The booklet also tells you how to learn to play the harmonica, beginning with the way to hold it, the knack of tonguing it, producing vibrato and artistic effects and, finally, playing it with a piano accompaniment. After you have read this little book you will be able to play the harmonica in a very short time and without any appreciable effort on your part.

The Accordion Hobby.—Before the advent of the phonograph the *accordion* [2] in its cheapest form was the musical instrument par excellence of the proletariat, and

[1] Another good book is the *Easy Method for the Harmonica,* published by Wm. J. Smith Music Co., Inc., N. Y.

[2] We get the name *accordion* from the Middle English *accord* which, in music, means the *harmony of sounds.*

thousands are still being made and sold every year. In recent times it has been developed into a magnificent instrument that costs as much as a piano, and as a thing of beauty and a joy forever it ranks a close second with the other and older classic instruments.

The accordion is really a gloriously glorified harmon-

FIG. 53.—THE PIANO ACCORDION AND HOW IT IS PLAYED

ica, for it likewise consists of two sets of tuned metallic reeds, each one of which is fixed to the frame of the instrument so that when a stream of air impinges on it, it will vibrate and so sound its proper tone. The great improvement of the accordion over the harmonica is that the reeds of the former are controlled by keys and the air that operates them is supplied by a bellows.

Kinds of Accordions.—There are two kinds of accordions and these are (*1*) the ordinary kind, and (*2*) the piano kind. The *ordinary accordions* are the German and the Vienna models; the former ranges in price from $7.00 for a *10*-key one having *2* basses, to $22.00 for a *21*-key one with four basses. The latter models are better made and range in price from $11.00 to $50.00. With these accordions you can get two tones from each key— one when you draw it out and one when you press it in.

The piano accordion [3] which is pictured in *Fig. 53* is the most remarkable portable musical instrument that has ever been invented for it is a whole orchestra in itself. It is a beautifully made instrument, of marvelous tone and, it follows, it will give you lasting enjoyment. The prices of these instruments range from $95.00 for one that has *25* piano keys and *24* basses, to $650.00 for one that has *41* piano keys, and *120* basses.

The right-hand keyboard is made like that of a piano and has a range of three octaves, while the latter has six octaves. The left-hand keyboard of the instrument has an entirely different set-up and it is the maze of buttons which form it that usually staggers the beginner. As a matter of fact, it is a comparatively easy keyboard to finger because you can play a chord by the pressure of a single button, whereas with the piano you have to use *4* or *5* fingers to play a chord. Also the left-hand keyboard of the instrument is so constructed that if you can play in one key the fingering is the same in all other keys regardless of the number of sharps and flats.

While piano accordions can be bought ready-made from dealers who sell musical instruments, the very best that money can buy are custom built. A high-grade

[3] So called because it has keys like a piano.

custom-built accordion costs in the neighborhood of $600.00, and it can be had of *The Excelsior Accordion Manufacturing Company*, Fourth Street and Sixth Avenue, New York City.

Learning to Play the Piano Accordion.—When you have made up your mind to learn to play the instrument, send for a booklet [4] called *The Art of Playing the Piano Accordion*, by C. Irving Valentine, to the *Rudolph Wurlitzer Company*, *121* East Fourth Street, Cincinnati, Ohio. This gives you a complete course of instruction that tells you exactly what you must know about the instrument and how to play it.

The booklet is divided into twelve lessons, the first of which tells you all about the instrument, how to hold it, the control of the bellows, gives various bass keyboard charts, first bass exercises, and a simplified method of playing a dozen or more songs, which you can do almost the first time you try.

There are a number of short-cuts and devices that have been invented by my clever young friend, John H. Reuther, of *618* West *143*rd Street, New York City, which will enable you to instantly understand and overcome some of the more difficult situations, whether you are a rank beginner or an experienced player. If you will write to him he will gladly give you a lot of valuable pointers that will be of great service to you.

The Musical Glasses Hobby.—The *musical glasses* make about the sweetest music that mortal man has ever been privileged to hear on this mundane sphere, or is ever likely to hear. As a hobby, the musical glasses have

---

[4] A copy of it is given free with every instrument that is sold, or *$1.50* if you buy it alone.

many good points in their favor, to wit, that you can make them yourself, they are quite inexpensive, easy to learn to play, you can play them as a solo instrument, or with the accompaniment of other instruments and, finally, you can play them for the beatification of your own sweet self, or the edification of a gathering of friends.

How to Make Them.—To make a simple set of musical glasses get eight very thin glass goblets and mount them on a board; to do this you need only to fasten the foot of each goblet down with a couple of thin strips of

FIG. 54.—THE MUSICAL GLASSES AND HOW THEY ARE PLAYED

tin or brass placed across it, and then screw the ends of these to the board as shown in *Fig. 54.*

To tune the glasses, pour water in them until each one has exactly the right pitch so the set will form an octave. When you have tuned the glasses to the *major scale,* that is the standard scale of eight tones to the octave, you can then play little tunes on them such as "Yankee Doodle," "Swanee River," "Old Black Joe," and other simple popular ones. When you have learned these tunes on an octave of musical glasses you can make a set of 22 glasses which will give you three octaves, and you can then play almost any of the popular airs.

How to Play Them.—The first thing to do in order to play the musical glasses is to moisten the rims of them with some water in which you have put a little vinegar, or better, *acetic acid,*[5] until when you rub your fingers over them they feel rough.

Now when you lay the tips of your fingers flat on the rim of a glass and rub them around on it, the friction between the skin of your roughened fingers and the edge of the glass will set the latter into vibration, and it will emit a wonderfully sweet tone. By varying the pressure of your fingers on the glasses you can produce a very beautiful *tremolo* effect.

It is a good scheme to put a few drops of acetic acid into each goblet, so that the moment the volume of sound begins to fall off as you rub the edge of it, you can dip your fingers into it (the goblet) without loss of time or the effort of reaching, and so increase the friction between them and the glass.

The Xylophone Hobby.—There is music in everything if you only know how to get it out of it. When a boy beats on a tin pan, or drums on a fence, he is making music of the *bombastic order,* and while he gets the keenest pleasure from the rhythmic sound thus set up it is just a pain in the cervical region to the grown-ups. This is because the sounds that he produces are a constant repetition of one or two tones.

Now a *xylophone* [6] (pronounced *zi'*-lo-fone) is an instrument that is formed of a series of wooden bars which

[5] This is the active acid of vinegar, which contains *4* to *12* per cent of it the rest being water.

[6] We get the word *xylophone* from the Greek roots *xulon,* which means *wood,* and *phone* meaning *sound.*

are graduated in length to the musical scale. These bars rest on rolls of straw and the tones are set up by striking them with a pair of small wooden hammers.

To play the xylophone, you take a hammer in each hand and hold it loosely by its handle. This done, stand over the xylophone so that the sticks of the hammers are parallel with, and about 4 or 5 inches above the wooden bars, with the ball on the end of each one in the middle of the bar it is over. Now hammer out the tune you are playing as though your very life depended on it, and the faster you play it the better it will sound. For this reason pieces like the *Circus Life Gallop* are best suited to the instrument.

The Metalophone.—This instrument is made like a xylophone except that the bars are formed of highly tempered steel, or of a special aluminum alloy, instead of wooden bars. When you play on these with cushioned mallets, they give very brilliant, captivating tones. *J. C. Deagan, Inc., 1770* Berteau Avenue, Chicago, Illinois, make two kinds of metalophones known as (*1*) orchestra bells and (*2*) vibraharps.

The *orchestra bells* are made in several different models, the smallest and cheapest one having *12* steel bars, ranging from *C* to *G* of the major scale and this costs *$4.50;* a larger set has *25* steel bars and a range of *2* chromatic octaves, that is from *C* to *C*, and this costs *$8.00.* The *vibraharp* is something else again for it has *37* aluminum bars, which gives *3* octaves, i. e., from F^6 to F^{42}, and these are fitted with resonators. The exotic tones that are produced by them are controlled by means of pulsator disks which are rotated by an electric motor;

these are operated by a foot pedal so that you can silence or sustain the tones at will. The instrument is made in various models and cost from *$295.00* to *$375.00*.

The Marimba.—A *resonator* is an open cylinder made of brass or other material, and it is so designed that it will

FIG. 55.—THE MARIMBA AND HOW IT IS PLAYED

concentrate and amplify a musical sound which is set up near one end of it by its resonance.[7] A South African tribe called the *A-Zandehs* make a kind of primitive xylophone which has gourds for resonators and this instrument they call a *marimba*.

[7] For a description of the way the resonator works see any textbook on college physics.

The *modern marimba* is a large and finely made xylophone with an accurately tuned metal resonator under each bar as shown in *Fig. 55*. These eliminate the harshness of the sounds that are given out when the bars are struck and deepen the organ tones of the bass; this blends with the sparkling treble, all of which make it the finest percussion instrument imaginable.

The Deagan Company also make a dozen, more or less, different models of the marimba, the cheapest of which has *37* bars, registers *3* octaves, from C^{25} to C^{61} and costs *$75.00*. The most expensive marimba that this firm makes has *56* bars, registers *4½* octaves, from F^6 to C^{61} and costs *$325.00*.

Learning to Play the Xylophone.—If you want to learn to play the xylophone quickly and without the aid of musical notation, you can use special guide strips and charts that are furnished with the instrument, when you can play it by numbers. The ease with which you can learn to play the xylophone by this scheme will amaze you.

A complete course of instruction is given free with each Deagan instrument, and this includes every phase of percussion musical instrument playing, from the fundamentals to the advanced work. If you will put in a reasonable amount of time you can learn to play any of the above instruments without any other instruction than that which is contained in these practical and easily understood lessons.

The Saxophone Hobby.—The *saxophone* is his Satanic Majesty's own instrument, but before I tell you how it is made and how to jazz it, I want you to know its diabolical history. First off, Satan's idea of a musical instrument was, naturally enough, one that looked like a serpent,[8] and so away back there in the pristine days when music was coming to the fore he inveigled one of his worldly disciples to make one and learn to play it.

This instrument, see *A* in *Fig. 56,* which was actually called a *serpent,* was made of a conical wooden tube that was curved and bent over on itself so that it looked

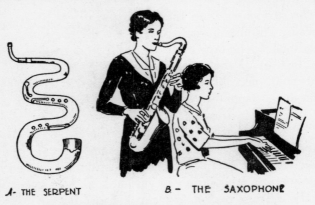

A- THE SERPENT   *B* - THE SAXOPHONE

Fig. 56.—The Saxophone and How It Is Played

as nearly as possible like a snake. It had a cupped mouth-piece on its small end, while the large end flared out like a trumpet. It was provided with finger-holes and when it was played it gave forth loud, harsh, bass tones that sounded as if the winds of Hades had broken loose.

The serpent was superseded by an instrument called the *ophicleide* (pronounced *of'*-i-cled), a word coined from the Greek *ophis* which means *serpent,* and *kgeis* meaning *key,* and it was so called because it was, in fee simple, our old friend Satan's serpent instrument, but

[8] Satan was often called the *Old Serpent.*

which had finger keys on it instead of just plain holes in it. When it was played it gave forth deep, powerful, resonant tones with a compass of about *3* octaves. The *tuba,* which is a deep toned saxhorn with from *3* to *5* valves, and giving the chromatic tones of nearly *4* octaves, has long since taken its place in bands and orchestras.

The *saxophone* is so called because it was invented in *1840* by Antoine Joseph Sax, a French musical instrument maker, and he got the idea of it from the ophicleide. But instead of the cupped mouthpiece on it he used a reed mouthpiece like that of the clarinet. It is played in orchestras, bands—especially military bands—and as a *hot cha* solo instrument. A good player can get sounds out of a saxophone such as the negroid tribes of Africa never heard, but he can also get some very intriguing music out of it that is decidedly pleasing, and which has a mesmeric attraction about it that makes it impossible for the average person to make his feet behave.

Kinds of Saxophones.—Saxophones are by no means cheap instruments, the lowest priced one being that of Martin, of Elkhart, Indiana. This goes by the name of *Home Model,* and its price is *$59.50.* It is a hand-built instrument and, as its name indicates, it is made especially for the hobbyist to have fun with in his own home. When it is played with a guitar, a banjo, piano, or a piano-accordion, or any combination of these instruments, you will have your own home orchestra, as at *B, Fig. 56.*

Wurlitzer makes a fine line of saxophones and these range in price from *$75.00* for a soprano instrument, *$80.00* for an alto, *$85.00* for a *C* melody, *$90.00* for a tenor, *$135.00* for a baritone, and *$200.00* for a bass one.

A very popular saxophone with its attachments is the *alto sax outfit* which costs *$92.00,* and the *C melody sax outfit* which sells for *$122.00.*

Learning to Play the Saxophone.—While the key arrangement of the saxophone appears on first sight to be quite complicated, it is really very simple. The keys are so placed that they fit your hands like a glove, and this enables you to play the most difficult music without changing the natural position of them.

If you are musically inclined you can learn to play the popular tunes from ordinary sheet music in two or three weeks. If not, then you will need a few lessons and these will start you off on the track of a musical education. You can get a world of pleasure out of a saxophone when you play it at home, and you can enjoy popularity plus whereever you go.

The Musical Saw Hobby.—It does seem a bit incredible, but it is nevertheless true, that a common saw makes a very good substitute for a fiddle. And very wonderful is the music that it makes when you play on it with a violin bow. Moreover, the musical saw (see *Fig. 57*) is very easy to learn and still easier to play, and here is how you do it.

How to Play the Saw.—To play the saw you must hold the handle of it firmly between your knees with the back edge of it away from you. Now grip the upper and free end of it with your left hand and bend it slightly in two opposing directions so that it curves like an elongated letter S. This done, take a well rosined violin bow, and move it forth and back on the edge of the saw, when it will give out appealing sounds something like a wailing human voice. The reason you can learn to play it easily is because you have only to bend the saw to a greater or lesser degree in order to get the note you want.

The Ukulele, Tiple and Taro Patches.—Ukulele (pronounced ö-koo-*lā'*-lā) is a Hawaiian word that means

FIG. 57.—THE MUSICAL SAW AND HOW IT IS PLAYED

a *flea*, or other jumping insect. The instrument is like a small guitar but instead of six strings like the latter, it has four strings. It has practically taken the place of the mandolin, except among the *gobs* of the Navy who still cling to the belly-shaped instrument.

There are numerous different styles of ukuleles, or just *ukes* as they are called for short, and these range in price from *$1.75,* which is one made of birch, and has friction wood pegs, to *$55.00,* which is one made of Hawaiian koa wood, elaborately decorated with mother-of-pearl and has an extra long scale. One model is shown at *A* in *Fig. 58.*

The *tiple* is an unusual instrument. Some of them are made like the ukulele and others like the guitar. However made, the tiple has *10* strings in four groups, and it is

A- THE UKULELE   *B-* THE BANJO-UKULELE
FIG. 58.—THE UKULELE AND THE BANJO-UKULELE

played like a ukulele. The price of it ranges from *$30.00* to *$75.00.* The body of the *taro patches* is made the same as a concert ukulele but it has four pairs of strings. You can get one made of mahogany for *$18.00,* or one of koa for *$28.00.*

The Banjo and Banjo Ukulele.—The good old banjo of way-down-south-in-the-land-of-cotton is still a prime favorite, and the twanging of it always reminds me of my boyhood days when the Negro minstrel was in flower.

The *banjo* gets its name from the French *bandore*, and it is clear that it is a corruption of the latter word through Negro slave mispronunciation.

As you well know, it is a stringed instrument that has a body like a tambourine and a neck like a guitar. It has five strings and you either pick them with your fingers or strike them with a plectrum.[9] About the cheapest banjo that is made costs *$7.50*, and from this prices soar on upward to *$375.00*. This latter style is fitted with a tonetube, or resonator, which gives it a very sweet and entrancing tone. The *banjo-ukulele,* which is shown at *B,* is a cute little instrument that is made like a banjo but is strung like a ukulele. The cheapest one costs only *$2.50* and the highest priced one *$8.75*.

To learn to play any of the foregoing stringed instruments get a copy of *Winn's Chord and Jazz Book,*[10] the price of which is *$1.00;* this shows you how to determine the correct chords to accompany any melody in any key, and to play the latest popular songs with melody and harmony combined (duo style) for piano sheet music. It also enables you to play up-to-date melodies and to accompany (harmonize) popular songs at once and, finally, how to *rag* and *jazz* music at sight.

The Trap Drum Hobby.—The *drum* is the most ancient of all of the musical hobbies and it is going stronger than ever before. It is a musical percussion instrument and consists of a hollow cylinder made of wood or metal, with a thin skin or vellum head stretched over each end, and these are held taut by either cords or

[9] This is a piece of ivory, wood, metal, horn or a quill that is used to strike strings with.
[10] You can get this book of the Rudolph Wurlitzer Company.

screws. It is played with a single stick or a pair of them, depending on the kind of drum it is.

Now there are two kinds of drums, and these are (*1*) the snare, or tenor drum and (*2*) the bass drum. You can get a snappy *snare drum* for home or school use with a

FIG. 59.—THE TRAP DRUM AND HOW IT IS PLAYED

pair of drumsticks for about *$8.00,* and, of course, a better one for more money. A *bass drum,* since it is much larger, naturally, costs considerably more, the cheapest being in the neighborhood of *$20.00.* It is, however, a *trap drum* outfit that will charge your mental battery until you can almost see the sparks fly and start up plenty at home.

The New Gang Outfit, which costs $35.00, consists of a junior snare drum, a junior bass drum, a drum stand, a light-weight drum pedal, with spurs and cymbal holder, an *8*-inch brass cymbal, a *10*-inch Chee Foo crash cymbal, a goose-neck crash cymbal holder, a Chinese redwood block, a wood block holder, a pair of hickory drum sticks, a pair of jazz brushes, and *Leedy's Beginner's Drum Method* which tells you how to use all of these things. The instruments are all shown in *Fig. 59.*

You can add mightily to the zest of your trap-drumming by getting one or more—the more the merrier—of the following devices; Spanish castanets, a gypsy tambourine, a Chinese tom-tom, a set of cowbells, a Chinese musette, which latter has a weird Oriental tone and, last, but not least, one or more imitating whistles.

These latter are (*a*) the cyclone whistle, (*b*) song whistle, (*c*) baby cry, (*d*) hen cackle, (*e*) Shanghai rooster crow, (*f*) steam exhaust, (*g*) bob-white, (*h*) cow bawl, and (*i*) a cuckoo whistle. You can get all of the above accessories and everything else that is cited in this chapter of The Rudolph Wurlitzer Company, *121* East Fourth Street, Cincinnati, Ohio, or at any one of its many branch stores in the United States.

CHAPTER X

A FEW AMUSEMENT HOBBIES

WHENEVER and wherever a number of your friends fore-gather for a social hour or two, there may come a brief period when the art of conversation lags, or mayhap, breaks down entirely, and the field finds itself running on a heavy track. When this happens it is your signal to come romping in on your piebald hobby and so save the day.

Now the hobbies I shall tell you how to ride in this chapter are rip-rarin' to go and they are as frisky as two-year-olds on a frosty morning. This being the way of it, they are calculated not only to give you a large meas-ure of fun and thrills but, and this is equally to the point, your friends as well, and all of this is done by the simple expedient of having them *listen to the professor.*

I have divided the hobbies in this chapter into two groups and these are (*1*) character reading, and (*2*) for-tune telling. *Character reading* is the act or art of guess-ing a person's mental traits or qualities by an examina-tion of a part or the whole of his physical make-up, or by his handwriting; and *fortune-telling* is the art or act of pretending to predict events that will come to pass in the life of a person.

Far be it from me to crack down on either of these good old hobbies, but you should know right here that neither of the above groups has the slightest scientific merit, for they are either founded on ancient ideas, or, and this is even worse, on false premises. Still, whether those whom you are amusing with your alleged readings take any stock in them or not, the primitive superstitions which urge that there may possibly be some truth in it, invariably crop out and the interest in your hobby never falters.

Character Reading Hobbies.—There are various means and schemes by which character reading is done, and chief among these are (*1*) phrenology, (*2*) palmistry, (*3*) physiognomy, (*4*) physical generalization and (*5*) graphology. Whichever one of these you choose as a hobby treat it just as you would any other and legitimate one—that is learn all about it you can, by reading books on the subject, and then practice it on anybody and everybody that comes your way. But be like the sundial, which tells only the sunshiny hours, that is tell the person whose character you are reading only the nice, pleasant and good traits about him and never those which are uncomplimentary.

The Hobby of Phrenology.—We get the word *phrenology* from the Greek roots *phron* which means *mind* and *logia* meaning *science,* that is, it means *mind science.* It is the art or practice of estimating a person's mental abilities and traits by examining the conformations or bumps of his cranium or skull. It is based on three erroneous suppositions: (*1*) that the bumps on the skull exactly agree with and, it follows, show the development of the brain that is immediately under them, (*2*) that the brain is divided into separate and distinct parts, each of which functions as a special faculty, and (*3*) that these have been accurately determined by Gall [1] who invented the system, and further developed by his associate, Spurzheim.

How to Begin.—To take up phrenology as a hobby you should study the chart shown in *Fig. 60* very care-

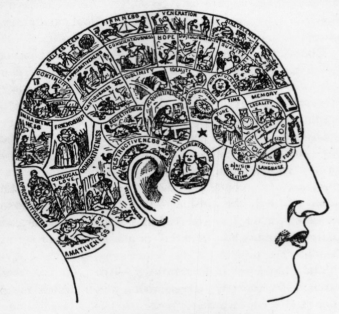

FIG. 60.—A CHART OF PHRENOLOGY

fully, which indicates where the various parts of the brain (according to Gall) are located. There are *35* circumscribed areas of the skull which correspond to the different organs of the brain, beginning with *amativeness,* which is the faculty that is supposed to influence sexual

[1] Franz Joseph Gall, a German physician who lived from *1758* to *1828*.

desire, to *causality,* which is the faculty that is supposed to trace effects to their causes.

When you have learned the names of all of the bumps and their relative positions on the skull your next move is to get a subject—preferably a man who has a head as bald as a hen's egg—and then locate the areas on it. After you have become proficient in finding the bumps and translating them into their respective faculties, you can tell with very little additional practice whether the bumps and, hence, the faculties, are under, fully, or over developed.

Having learned all of the above things, you are then a full-fledged phrenologist and to acquire the necessary technique for giving an exhibition of your hobby, you must *phrenologize,* that is, examine the heads of every one you can. This you do by placing your forefingers and middle fingers of both hands on the subject's skull and explore the undulating surface of it carefully. There are any number of books on phrenology, and you should read one or more of them—it doesn't much matter which for, in the last analysis, one is just about as good as the other.

The Hobby of Palmistry.—*Palmistry* (pronounced *pom'*-is-tri) is a word compounded from the Greek root *palam* which means *hand,* and the old French noun *maistrie* meaning *mastery* or *skill.* Palmistry is the art or practice of (*1*) judging the traits and aptitudes, and (*2*) the past and possible future of a person from his hand. The art is based on the shape of the hand itself and especially on the lines, marks and mounts in the palm of it.

The *lines* are supposed to indicate the disposition, affections, passions and fortunes of a person. The *marks* show the various individual characteristics, while the *mounts,* or eminences, which are named after the planets,[2] denote the temperament or predominant traits. From the above you will see that palmistry, like phrenology, is

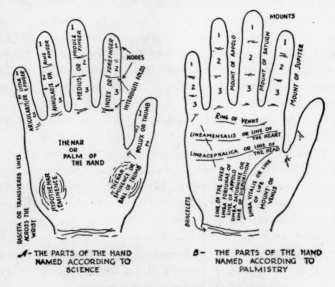

A - THE PARTS OF THE HAND NAMED ACCORDING TO SCIENCE

B - THE PARTS OF THE HAND NAMED ACCORDING TO PALMISTRY

Fig. 61.—Reading Palms for Fun

a mild sort of bunkum squint, but for entertaining a party of friends it can't be beaten as a fun-maker.

How to Begin.—There are two things that you should learn before you begin to read palms (pronounced *poms*), and these are (*1*) the names of the different parts of the hand, and (*2*) the lines and mounts of it. I have shown and named the parts of the hand according to science at

[2] These were so named because they were believed to be indicative of the influence of the planets upon the person.

A in *Fig. 61,* and the parts of the hand named according to palmistry, at *B.* Calling the parts of the hand by their scientific lines, and the lines and the mounts by their pseudo-scientific or palmistry names is quite impressive to those who know nothing about the art.

You are now ready to read the palm of any one who wants you to—but don't let him or her "cross your palm with silver" according to the old gypsy custom, or you may find yourself in the clutches of the law. But palmistry for entertainment purposes only is O.K. The main thing in reading palms is to talk fluently and build up a lively description of a person's character by what you think the lines and the mounts reveal, or ought to reveal.

The Hobby of Physiognomy.—The word *physiognomy* (pronounced *fiz'*-e-og-no-my) is compounded from the Greek roots *phuois* which means *nature* and *gnomun* meaning to *judge*. It is the art or practice of judging the temperamental characteristics of the mind and other mental attributes from the features of the face.

It is curious, but nonetheless true, that all of us, regardless of age, race, creed or color, has exactly the same mental picture of what a person is like by the features of his face. Thus we all know what the godly man, and the villain, who forged the will in the blacksmith shop, the hard but just man and the meek and henpecked one, the minister, and the gunman, look like or, at least, ought to look like. This is proved by the fact that actors always make up to look like the part of the characters they are playing.

How to Start.—This being the way of it, you can readily see that physiognomy is far from being a science. Now there are two ways by which you can read a per-

son's character from his face and these are to (*1*) interpret his disposition and traits by depending on your im-
pressionistic sense, that is as you see and feel them, and
(*2*) which does not give any better results, is to use the
method formulated by Johannes Kaspar Lavater,[3] a
Swiss clergyman and artist, and this will require considerable study on your part. The scheme he devised was
to take portraits of all the well-known personages of his
time, and knowing what their mental attributes were, he
laid down rules for connecting up the shapes of the features with them. Thus the shapes of the eyes, nose,
mouth, ears and chin were associated with ambition,
goodness, firmness, disposition and sensuality.

The Duality Mirror.—A curious thing about the human
face is that it is *two-sided*, that is, each half of it looks very
different from the other half. To see this difference to the
best advantage you must use a *duality mirror*, that is, a
thin strip of metal which is polished to mirror brilliancy on
both sides. It was invented and patented by my friend
William E. Benton, *323* West *53*rd Street, New York
City.

To use it you place one of its edges over a full-faced
picture of the person whose dual character you are going
to read, as shown at *A* in *Fig. 62*. Now when you look at
one half of the picture from one side you will see at the
same time a reflection of it in the mirror and this forms
the image of a full front view. As you examine it you will
observe that the person has an honest, sympathetic, intellectual look, while the other side shows a character of an
entirely different kind, and this is often secretive, sensuous
and cruel.

[3] He lived from *1741* to *1801*.

This Jekyll and Hyde quality, see *B*, is not necessarily in itself bad, but it depends on the person's control of them. Thus when it is employed for the benefit of humanity it is called good and noble and, conversely, when it is employed for evil purposes, it is called wicked and depraved.

A- THE LEFT SIDE OF THE REV. MR. X's FACE

Right side of face mirrored indicates the conscious, or obvious, side of his nature was sensitive, intellectual, cultured, persuasive, honest and direct.

Left side of face mirrored reveals that the subconscious, or hidden nature of the Rev. Dr. X was secretive, sullen, cruel destructive and sensuous.

B- A MR. JEKYLL AND MR. HYDE
The Rev. Mr. X

FIG. 62.—A MIRROR FOR READING THE FACE

The Scientific Aspect of Physiognomy.—Physiognomy has a scientific aspect and this has to do, not with individual traits, disposition and emotions, but with the comparative characteristics of the races, the traits of blondes and brunettes, of long heads and round heads, etc. This branch of physiognomy makes a very interesting, scientific hobby, but it has no value from the entertainment stand-point.

The Hobby of Physical Generalization.—By *physical generalization* is meant the art or practice of reading character by *sizing up* the person. When you scrutinize a person, i. e., look him over from head to foot, you instantly get, or think you get, the *lowdown* on not only his mental attributes and physical characteristics, but also his financial status.

The more acute your powers of observation are, the more you can gather about the individual whom you are reading. This, in a nutshell, is the Sherlock Holmes method of deduction which was made famous by the late Conan Doyle in his stories of the great legendary detective, and it is a great success, especially if you happen to be acquainted with the individual whom you are reading.

How to Begin.—The first thing to do is to (*1*) make a note of the person's general appearance, (*2*) the kind of clothes he wears and how he wears them, (*3*) his facial characteristics, (*4*) his actions, and (*5*) his speech and the subjects he talks on. If he is well-dressed and well-groomed, you will naturally believe that he is prosperous; on the other hand, if he wears an old suit and this is unpressed, if he is unshaven and has not had the daily shower or bath, you are certainly within the bounds of good judgment to believe that he is provisionally *broke*.

All of this seems to be a fair and logical deduction but the trouble with it is that there are a few bus-boys and other menial servants who are immaculate fashion-plates when they are off duty, and, likewise, a few capitalists in the millionaire class who wear the same suit of clothes for ten years, more or less. If it were not for these off-color, ten-to-one shots who do not run true to form, then physical generalization would approximate an exact science, instead of being an abrupt science, as Artemus Ward used to say.

However, practically all character readers and fortune tellers get their highlights on their patrons by giving their physical make-up and other personal characteristics the once over. Although physical generalization is full of errors, still it makes a most interesting hobby either for your own pleasure or for the entertainment of your friends.

The Hobby of Graphology.—From the ancient Greek roots *graphos* which means *to write* and *logia* meaning a *science,* we get the compound word *graphology* and this, in turn, means the art or practice of judging a person's character and traits by a study of his handwriting. Like the character reading schemes that have gone before, graphology is a pseudo-science, and, therefore, you must not take it too seriously, but only as a light, pleasure-giving entertainment hobby.

That the handwriting does indicate the mental and physical capacities of a person there is no doubt and, hence, it would seem that it ought to be possible to interpret, at least roughly, his mental caliber and physical mannerisms by it; the reason that this cannot be done, however, is due to the fact that the multiplicity of factors involved cannot be systematized and, therefore, used with anything like an approximation of accuracy.[4]

[4] The following are two good books on graphology. *Mind Your P's and Q's,* by Jerome S. Meyer, published by Simon and Schuster, New York, and *Psychology of Handwriting,* by William French, published by G. P. Putnam's Sons, New York.

How to Begin.—The way to begin graphology is to get a book on the subject, and the first thing to learn is (*1*) what the general features of handwriting are, and then (*2*) the special features of it and what they are. The general features are (*a*) the style, (*b*) the scope, (*c*) the size, (*d*) the form, (*e*) the speed, (*f*) the spacing, (*g*) the lines, (*h*) the margins, (*i*) the terminals, (*j*) the punctuation, (*k*) the capitals, and lastly (*l*) the signature.

The special features that you must know the meaning of include (*a*) the abducent and adducent writing, (*b*) connected and disconnected letters, (*c*) increasing, decreasing and variable-sized letters, (*d*) touched up letters, (*e*) initial strokes, (*f*) muddy writing, (*g*) small letters pointed at the top, (*h*) small letters rounded at the top, (*i*) divergent letters, (*j*) loop letters, and the (*k*) individual small letters. Albert J. Smith's *Applied Graphology,* published by the Gregg Publishing Company, New York and London, explains in detail all of the above features.

When you have learned the meaning of all of them you will be ready to qualify as a full-fledged graphologist, by which I mean that you can take a sample of a person's handwriting and, according to the rules of the game, you will be able to reveal all of his or her habits, traits and qualifications, to your own satisfaction, and the beautiful part of it is that no one can say you nay.

Some Fortune-Telling Hobbies.—*Fortune-telling* is the ancient and dishonorable art or practice of professing to reveal certain future events that will take place in the life of a person. It is truly surprising how many people in all walks of life believe in fortune-telling. Perhaps I have placed the estimate too high but it is my private opinion, publicly expressed, that nine out of every ten persons have implicit faith in it. And I have also observed that the tenth one is always quite willing to have his told "just for the fun of it," of course.

Be that as it may, fortune-telling when it is done by a hobbyist who has a sense of the fitness of things, a highly colored imagination, a fluent tongue and a ready wit, is one of the most interesting and entertaining diversions for passing away the time that has yet been invented.

Now there are numerous ways by which you can tell fortunes, the chief ones of which are by (1) astrology, (2) palmistry, (3) crystal-gazing, (4) cards, and (5) tea leaves. What I have told you about character reading schemes as hobbies holds equally well for fortune-telling hobbies. While fortune-telling by any one of the above means can be made the source of great interest and much merriment, it can also do a lot of harm unless you use a little hobby-horse sense.

Never, under any circumstances, tell a person that he, or any member of his family, is going to be sick, or have an accident, or that there will be a death in the family, and never urge any one, especially an old person, to have his fortune told—so strong is the belief in the thing! Whatever scheme you use, let your formula be the same, and that is to tell the subject that he will live to a ripe old age, there is oodles of money coming to him, he will make a long journey, a red-headed lady will try to do him wrong, he will sleep in a strange bed, and all of the rest of the happiness bunk. And now let's find out just how to ride these piebald hobbies.

The Hobby of Astrology.—We get the impressive

word astrology from the Greek roots *astron* which means
star; and *logos* meaning *discourse*, or, more freely trans-
lated, *to speak*. Astrology treats of the supposed influences of the stars on human affairs and, it follows, of
foretelling a person's future by their positions and aspects. In telling fortunes by astrology you do not make
an offhand verbal statement of your alleged deductions,
but you cast a horoscope for the person, or *native*, as he
or she is called.

To do this awe-inspiring thing you should know about
(*1*) the zodiac, and the nature of the planetary aspects
that take place in it; (*2*) the houses and the character
and purpose of each one; (*3*) the nature of the signs and
the sun and moon in the different ones; (*4*) the planets
and the influence of each one, and (*5*) the horoscope and
how to erect it.

The zodiac is an imaginary belt in the heavens that is
16 degrees wide, the middle line of which is called the
ecliptic, and this is the path of the sun. It includes 12 divisions, or houses, as the astrologer calls them; originally
these were named after the constellations that were in
them, beginning with Aries, the Ram, and ending with
Pisces, the Fishes, as pictured at *A* in *Fig. 63*. Due to the
precession of the equinoxes the houses have separated
some *30* degrees for these constellations, and each of the
latter now lies in the former one next ahead of it; thus
the constellation of Aries is now in the house of Taurus,
etc.

It is the planet or planets that are in these houses, and
their relative positions in them when a person is born
that are supposed to influence his life until he finally

catches up with old Father Time; this gives you a clue
to the fortune of the person whose fortune you are telling.

The houses are considered to be fixed in reference to
the horizon and numbered from one at the eastern horizon, which is called the ascendant, first house, or house
of life, downward, that is in the direction of the earth's
revolution, the stars and the planets passing them in the
reverse order every *24* hours as it affects the person or

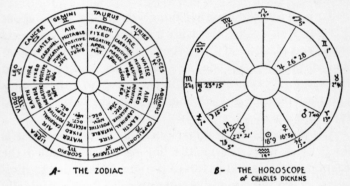

A- THE ZODIAC   B- THE HOROSCOPE
                        of CHARLES DICKENS

Fig. 63.—The Zodiac and a Horoscope

native. Each house has its especial influence, and these
have to do with his personal qualities such as his disposition, self-interest, monetary and financial prospects,
speculation, love, pleasure, marriage, partnership, legal
affairs, long journeys, possible troubles, *terminus vitæ*,
which means death, and the result of it on wills, legacies,
executorships, and what have you.

The signs of the zodiac control the physical being of
the individual as, for instance, the first sign Aries which
indicates the Ram, and is ♈; this has to do with

the head and face, while the last sign, which indicates Pisces, the Fishes, and is ♓, takes care of the feet; the signs of all of the other houses run the gamut of the parts of the physical body that are in between these two extremities.

As the sun and the moon pass through the various signs of the zodiac, the character of the individual will be affected accordingly.

The planets have been designated by the astrologers to be the real rulers of the destiny of man and where these are in certain positions in the zodiac, they are said to be exalted, or in detriment, as the case may be. Thus Venus is the goddess of love and, hence, she governs all that is agreeable and lovely, all that is sweet and pleasant, and all of the pleasures and amusements of the person who is born under her influence.

On the other hand, Mars is the god of war and this shows that the individual who is born under him is rash, precipitate, proud and overbearing, with the consequent result that he is particularly liable to quarrels, assaults, accidents, disease and surgical operations. In a like manner, each of the other planets have their especial dispensations, and these affect the future of the individual.

The horoscope is the *it* in astrology and when you can erect one, which means that you cast or make it so that it shows what the celestial condition is of the person who was born under it, and how it influences his future, you will be ready to make your bow among the intelligentsia as an astrologer, and be acclaimed by the diverse members of it as a mystery man, or woman, who can read the judgments of the mortals here below, in and by the light of the distant stars.

The word *horoscope* comes from the Greek roots *oros* which means *boundary* and *skopio, to view,* and, in a larger sense, to see or observe the hour of birth and the influence of the stars and planets on the person. The horoscope, see *B,* is, simply, a kind of a map of the heavens. Now there are two kinds of horoscopes used by astrologers: (*1*) the square map, and (*2*) the round map. In making, or erecting, a horoscope of the heavens for any given moment of time, on any particular date, the first thing you must have is an astronomical table called an *ephemeris,* and second a book on *astrology,*[5] and you can get these of any dealer in occult books.

Having read these make a schema or diagram, of the *12* signs or houses of the zodiac and this you do by drawing a square or a circle and dividing it into *12* equal parts, as shown at *B.*

This done ascertain the exact time of the individual's birth, and from the ephemeris find the positions of the sun, moon and planets in the houses or signs at that particular moment. Mark the positions of these on the horoscope and then consult your book on astrology and write out the chief events that correspond with them. When in doubt guess out the forthcoming events for they will be just as likely to be correct as the most learned and dignified astrologist can come to it with all his masterful occult knowledge.

The Hobby of Palmistry.—In the first part of this chapter I explained that palmistry is employed not only for character reading, but for fortune-telling as well. To use it for the latter purpose you should learn the names

[5] The Macoy Publishing Co., *35* West *32*nd Street, New York City, sells them.

of the lines, the marks, and the mounts on the hand, and the future events they are supposed to indicate,[6] and then use your intuition.

Fortune-telling by reading the palm of a person's hand has long been the chief method of the gypsies, but before they can see through the misty veil of your future, you must cross their palms with silver; and it is truly surprising how much some of them can see when you perform this plebeian act of superstition; and you can see as much as they without the token if you have sufficient intuition and vivid imagination.

The Hobby of Cardiology.—By *cardiology* is meant the scheme of telling fortunes by cards, and these may be either (*1*) playing cards, or (*2*) special cards, i. e., cards that are made for the purpose. There are numerous ways to tell fortunes with cards but all of them are based on the same fundamental idea and this is that each card in the pack has a bearing on, or indicates an event which will take place in the life of a person.

With Playing Cards.—Thus the ace of clubs promises great wealth; the king of diamonds shows a man of fiery temper who seeks revenge; the queen of hearts a fair and beautiful blonde, or one who has a high temper, and who is bent on making trouble; the jack of spades is not a knave, as you might well believe, but a man who has your interests at heart, or wants to protect you, etc.[7]

---

[6] There are numerous books on the art of palmistry that give you all of this misinformation and these sell for *10* cents on up to *$5.00* each. The cheap booklets will give you as good a run for your money as the higher priced books.

[7] For the meaning of each card in the pack, you must get a book on fortune-telling, or cardiology as it is termed, and there are plenty to choose from. The Curtis Publishing Co., Philadelphia (*Ladies' Home*

After you have learned the meaning of every card in the pack, an easy way to tell a person's fortune is to have him or her shuffle it and then choose *32* cards from it at random. This done you take *4* of these cards, or frame as it is called, at a time and knowing what each one means you build up a connected story of them. Then take up the next four cards and do the same thing with them, and so on until you have run through all of them.[8]

With Special Cards.—Special fortune-telling cards are, simply, a pack of cards of the regulation size, but having the indication of a future event printed on the face of each one, instead of pips and pictures as the regulation pack has. With a pack of this kind, all you have to do is to shuffle the cards and lay them out face up in rows on a table.

Beginning at the left-hand end, you read the text that is printed on each one and couple them together in a running story as nearly as you can. Of course you supplement the text by guesses of your own, otherwise the fortune of every one and his brother would be just alike. You can get a pack of these cards for *10* or *20* cents in any of the chain stores, with directions for various ways of reading them.

The Hobby of Crystal-Gazing.—As a spectacular variant of fortune-telling, *crystal-gazing* has all of the others locked in a vault. To perform the miracle of seeing the future in a glass clearly, all you need is a glass

---

Journal), published a booklet in 1934, called *Fortune-Telling*, which has a very good chapter on telling fortunes with cards.

[8] A booklet called the *Mystic Oracle and Complete Fortune-Teller*, published by I. & M. Ottenheimer, Baltimore, Md., will give you the meaning of each card, or you can dope them out for yourself if you care to go to the trouble of doing so.

ball that is about *3* inches in diameter which should be mounted on a little black stand or pedestal about *3* inches high.

If you cannot get a glass ball easily, you can use a small round glass fish bowl instead, turn it upside down, and conceal the mouth of it with a black cloth. The only other things you need are a fresh and lively tongue and a soothsayer's imagination. And you must not be afraid

FIG. 64.—A CRYSTAL-GAZING SÉANCE

to handle the truth carelessly. To make your readings still more impressive, you can dress like an Oriental seer, i. e., put on a fanciful robe and wrap a turban round your head.

When you are ready to see what the future holds in store for a person, have him or her sit on one side of a small table on which the crystal ball rests, and you seat yourself on the opposite side of it, as pictured in *Fig. 64.* Then gaze with soulful eyes into the ball and start off your predictions by saying, "Across the borderland, I see—" and then go on and describe a mystical fortune, a trip to Egypt, Japan or round the world, strange adventures, a handsome man (if your subject is a she) or a beautiful platinum blonde (if he's a he), romantic love, obstacles galore, but which are all happily surmounted, and, finally, a joyous wedding.

The Hobby of Reading Tea Leaves.—The most popular form of fortune-telling at the present moment is by reading tea leaves. This art belongs exclusively to the ladies, though, you will, of course, find an occasional male essaying the rôle, but it is not for virile man.

Now there are two ways to read fortunes by tea leaves, and these are (*1*) to learn set answers to the various shapes you picture that they make, and (*2*) and this is a great deal easier, and quite as effective, I assure you, is to use your imagination and intuition only. Whichever scheme you use, the person whose fortune you are going to tell must drink all of the tea in her cup, turn it upside down on the saucer and let it drain until only the leaves remain. He or she then turns the cup round three times and makes a wish.

This done you take the cup, gaze deeply into its depths (see *Fig. 65*), and seek out the various shapes that the leaves take. With your brilliant imagination, you will see that they assume a lot of familiar forms, such as geometrical figures, animals of all kinds, and numerous objects. When you see three leaves in a line it means his or her wish will come true; a number of small leaves in a line means a journey; triangles, flowers, trees and crowns are good luck signs, while crosses, snakes, and swords mean bad luck, etc.

Special formations of tea leaves have significant meanings; thus, a horse's head means a lover; a cat, treachery; a monkey, deceit; a dove, success in love and great good fortune; a peacock, a wedding, etc. If you don't want to take the time and go to the trouble of memorizing

FIG. 65.—READING YOUR FORTUNE IN TEA LEAVES

all of these little details you can go ahead and rattle off fortunes by the same artifice that I described for crystal-gazing. In telling fortunes by any of the above schemes, all I can say is to go to it and let your imagination be your guide.

CHAPTER XI

A FEW ENTERTAINMENT HOBBIES

THERE are various *vaudeville acts* that make the liveliest kinds of hobbies, and these you can do before a small private gathering or a large public audience. These acts are (*1*) a Punch and Judy show, (*2*) paper magic, (*3*) lightning crayon pictures, (*4*) juggling, balancing and spinning, (*5*) ventriloquism and vocal mimicry, (*6*) sleight-of-hand and magic, (*7*) shadowgraphs and silhouettes, (*8*) chapeaugraphy, (*9*) marionettes, (*10*) second sight and mental magic, (*11*) mind-reading, (*12*) animal magnetism and hypnotism, and (*13*) a spiritualistic séance.

I shall describe these various hobbies quite briefly, for the way to begin them, the things you need to do them with, and the way to do them, are all fully described in my *Book of Magic, The Amateur Entertainer* and *Making Things for Fun.*[1]

A Punch and Judy Show.—This is, as you well know, a puppet show, in which the principal characters are *Punch,* a misanthrope, and Judy, his far from amiable wife. Both of them are humpbacked, and to add to their grotesque appearance, they have enormous hooked noses. They speak with a squeaky voice, which is highly amusing because the sound is quite unlike that ever made by

[1] All of these are published by D. Appleton-Century Company, N. Y.

any of the members of the *Genus homo* and, it follows, it must belong to the land of make-believe.

To give the show you need (*1*) a framework that con-

FIG. 66.—A PUNCH AND JUDY SHOW

tains the stage, (*2*) the figures of Punch and Judy, and other characters, (*3*) a stick, gallows, coffin and other properties, (*4*) a Punch and Judy squeaker, and (*5*) a dialogue and the business that goes with it, which you must learn. The heads of the figures are made of *papier mâché,* or of wood if you buy them, or you can make them yourself of cloth.[2] To work them you slip your index finger into one sleeve and your thumb into the other one; you can then grasp the stick, or anything else, just as though the little arms are really living members— which they are for the time being. *Fig. 66* shows a Punch and Judy show in action.

A Paper Magic Act.—This consists of doing a variety of things with a sheet of paper, and these can be conveniently divided into three parts: (*1*) paper folding, (*2*) paper tearing, and (*3*) paper tricks.[3] It is surprising how many curious objects you can make by the simple expedient of *folding a sheet of paper,* and it is one of the finest ideas ever concerned with which to amuse children.

While *paper tearing* is a very old art and an exceedingly simple one, still it has been found of sufficient merit, when it is expertly performed, to be classed as a vaudeville act. Finally, tricks with paper are among the very easiest to do, and they are, at the same time, exceptionally brilliant and equally as deceptive as any that can be performed with expensive objects.

Among the *paper folds* that you can do is to make a soldier's hat, a drill baton, an officer's cap, a sailboat, a dart, a pinwheel, etc. By *tearing* and *cutting paper* you can make a ship's wheel, Brownies and dolls, a Jacob's ladder, etc., and of *paper tricks* there is the pair of Dickey birds, paper ribbons, Afghan bands, magic pocket book, the American flag, etc.

The Lightning Crayon Artist.—A highly pleasing and quite clever hobby is drawing cartoons and making

---

[2] The way to do this is explained in my *Making Things for Fun.*
[3] All of these acts are described in my *Amateur Entertainer.*

lightning crayon pictures.[4] Both of these specialties are very easy to do, and you can get by with them even if you don't know anything about drawing, while if you do they are easy plus.

The *cartoons,* so called, are of two kinds, (*1*) caricatures of the different races, and (*2*) portraits of well-known people, as Washington, Lincoln and Roosevelt. *Lightning crayon sketches* consist of drawing highly colored scenes with crayons on large sheets of paper in a jiffy, and because you execute them in a minute or two, your friends give you more than the share of credit which is really due you. Then again, a little distance between you and the spectators lends enchantment to your work.

Juggling, Balancing and Spinning.—These various acts are often performed singly, but they all fit in well together.[5] *Juggling* is the hardest of these hobbies to learn, *spinning* comes next, and *balancing* is the easiest. In all of these hobbies you make use of certain laws of nature, the chief ones being gravity, centrifugal force and air resistance.

When the feats are legitimately performed they require a lot of skill and to do them adroitly, a considerable amount of practice. You can use specially prepared apparatus for some of the feats and this greatly reduces the needed skill. The spectators of course know nothing of these subterfuges, and so you can do marvelous feats with little or no practice.

The Art of Juggling.—If you decide to take up jug-

---

[4] Both of these acts are fully described in my *Amateur Entertainer.*

[5] You will find all you need to know about them in *The Amateur Entertainer.*

gling as a hobby you can begin by learning how to toss up one ball, then two balls, and then to keep three balls going all at once. When you have acquired the knack of juggling three balls, you can do so with four balls, which is not so easy, and then to *shower* five and six balls at a time; this takes a lot of hard practice but when you can do so you will be able to juggle plates, bottles, Indian clubs, parasols and any other objects you may care to.

The Art of Balancing.—Balancing makes a mighty pretty hobby, and it consists of supporting some unstable object, from a feather to a chair, on some part of your body and keeping it from falling by counteracting movements, so that it will maintain its upright position. Gravity and air resistance are the chief forces that act on the object you are balancing, and the main thing for you to remember is that the lower the center of gravity in an object, the easier it is for you to keep it in a state of balance. You can begin by balancing a strip of paper on your nose, then a paper cone, a high hat, a chair, and other like objects.

The Art of Spinning.—Spinning can be done either by skill alone or by using specially prepared objects. Whichever you use, you should practise enough to get the fundamental principles of it down pat. By mixing an ounce of skill with a pound of subterfuge you can make possible some seemingly impossible feats.

The easiest way to learn to spin flat objects is to begin with a cheese-box lid, as this is comparatively large, rough and heavy, and it follows, it will be less likely to slip off of your finger when it is spinning. A little practice will enable you to keep the lid spinning on your finger, and when you can do so, you are ready to spin a tambourine, *à la* the endman in a minstrel show, a plate, or other flat, disk-shaped object.

You can buy plates and bowls that are made with concave bottoms so that it takes a minimum of skill to keep them spinning on the end of a stick. By pushing the blunt end of a needle in one end of a stick, you can keep a large handkerchief spinning, and if you have a top with a loose, grooved ferrule on the end of it, you can spin it on the edge of a sword or a wire that is kept in a horizontal position.

Vocal Mimicry and Ventriloquism.—The term *vocal mimicry* is used to mean the art of imitating sounds that are made by various insects, birds and mammals. If you have a very little native ability you will find it quite an easy matter to mimic the sounds of nearly all of the common animals, various musical instruments and household implements of different kinds. Thus, by vocal mimicry you can make the identical sound of a blue-bottle fly, the e-iow of a cat, the bark of a dog, and the crow of a rooster; the twanging of a banjo, the ta-ta-ta of a cornet, the zooming of a bass-viol, the pur-up, pur-up, pur-up, tup, tup of a tenor drum, the boom, boom of a bass drum, the clashing of the cymbals and, finally, the sawing of a stick of wood, the pulling of a cork, and the gurgling noise of drinking soda water from the bottle.

Ventriloquism is the pleasing art of mimicing the vocal sounds of various animals, especially those of the human family, and having them apparently come, not from your own mouth, but from a distant point. To be able to mimic a boy or a girl, a man or a woman, without any apparent motion of your lips depends to a large extent on your

natural ability, but with or without it you can learn to do
so.

In order to give your hobby a proper setting, you
should have a *ventriloquial dummy,* that is a figure whose
lower jaw is movable, and which you work by a concealed
lever with your finger as shown in *Fig. 67.* Now as you

FIG. 67.—A VENTRILOQUIAL ACT

talk and sing in a voice that is supposed to come forth
from the dummy, and synchronously move its jaw, it
will seem to the spectators who are at some little distance
away, as if the sounds came from it and not from yourself.

Sleight-of-Hand and Magic.—You can give a passably
good magical performance with a modicum of skill and
a minimum of apparatus if you know how to go about

it.[6] As an illustration, there are quite a number of tricks that make use of various schemes and subterfuges, and by using these you can do a *15-* or *20*-minute turn without having to go through a long siege of practice.

To make magic a real hobby, though, you must be a clever sleight-of-hand performer, that is to know how to make passes, manipulate coins, cards, balls, handker-

FIG. 68.—GIVING A PERFORMANCE OF MAGIC

chiefs, and other small objects, in order to make them appear and disappear at will, and there are no short cuts to learning how to do so.

If you will get my *Book of Magic* you will find in it just what you should know about magic and sleight-of-hand to make a hobby of them. (See *Fig. 68.*) It tells you how to do a lot of tricks, (*1*) without any skill or

[6] My *Book of Magic* tells you just how to do it. Send to Max Hoffman, 42nd Street, New York City, for his magical catalogue of apparatus, etc.

apparatus, (2) without skill and some simple apparatus, (3) with some skill and some apparatus, and, finally, (4) with skill only—which is pure sleight-of-hand.

Now as I have said in the preface of my book, if you like magic and will practise any sleight or trick for *30* minutes every day for a month you will be surprised to find how well you can do it. By putting together a few tricks and diligently practising them along with the necessary patter, or *talkee-talkee* as the Great Herrmann used to call it, you will be able to give a performance for your friends that will, as my good friend, Harry Kellar, used to say, baffle the senses, astound the mind, and mystify the human brain.

Shadowgraphs and Silhouettes.—These are novelty hobbies and they consist of throwing shadows of various objects on a screen. *Shadowgraphs* are shadows made by letting the light fall on cardboard or tin cut-outs, while *silhouettes* are shadows made by letting the light fall on your hands that are given the form of animals and faces. The former require only a little practice to give a show and, hence, are chiefly of interest to children, while the latter needs a lot of practice and, it follows, the show is suitable for all ages.

Mechanical shadowgraphs are made so that the shadows they cast will have various realistic movements as, for instance, the whale swallowing Jonah (or you can have Jonah swallowing the whale just as easy), Sambo riding the trick mule, as shown at *A* in *Fig. 69,* and ships that break in two and sink in a blaze of red fire.[7]

Animated shadows [8] are those made by casting the shad-

7 This is described in my *Book of Magic.*
8 See my *Making Things for Fun.*

ows of human beings on a screen. These animated shadowgraphs are easily produced and you can get some wonderful effects that will provoke no end of merriment.
Among these are shadows of people who jump up to

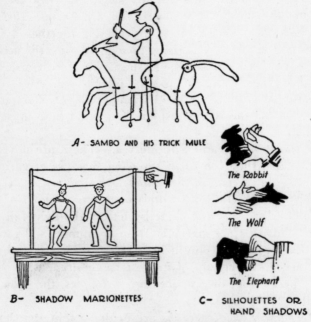

A— SAMBO AND HIS TRICK MULE

The Rabbit

The Wolf

The Elephant

B— SHADOW MARIONETTES

C— SILHOUETTES OR
HAND SHADOWS

FIG. 69.—SHADOWGRAPHS AND SILHOUETTES

the ceiling, painless extraction without gas, in which a
huge aching tooth is pulled out by an overzealous dentist
who uses a pair of blacksmith's tongs, etc.

Shadow marionettes [9] are a clever modification of real
marionettes and these are figures made of cardboard with

___

[9] See my *Amateur Entertainer.*

jointed arms and legs, which are worked by a thread. With these little shadow creatures you can give a most delightful and mysterious performance. The way to do it is pictured at *B*.

Silhouettes, or *hand shadows* [10] are easy to make as far as the mere making of them goes, but to become a graceful and rapid worker is something else again, and to attain a high degree of skill requires ability plus a great deal of practice. After you have had some experience making various animals (see *C*), you can then have a try at head silhouettes, including the man with the contractile nose.

Some very funny effects can be had by making your fingers represent full-length people and using little cardboard *props* to lend realism to the scene. Thus there is the *Lone Fisherman;* by raising and lowering your thumb, to which is attached a wire representing a pole and line, a fish will appear from and then disappear in the imaginary water. *The Street Musician* is a cute little silhouette in which an irascible old man in a nightcap pours water on an itinerant young man who is playing a flageolet under his window. There is very little expense to producing either shadowgraphs or silhouettes and they make the finest kind of hobbies.

Chapeaugraphy or Hat Impersonations.—*Chapeaugraphy* (pronounced chap-e-*og'*-ra-fi) is a novelty hobby [11] invented and performed by the great Trewey, and it comes from the French word *chapeau* which means *hat,* and the Greek suffix *graph* meaning *to write.* It consists of impro-

---

[10] See my *Book of Magic* and *Amateur Entertainer.*
[11] All of the details of this unusual hobby are explained in *The Amateur Entertainer.*

vising different shaped hats from a ring of felt and making various expressions to fit them.

All you need to do a chapeaugraphy act with is a ring of flexible felt [12] which you can bend and twist into various shapes. To lend verisimilitude to the different characters you present you should also have some false moustaches, a couple of beards and a cloak. To give an acceptable performance you must learn to change the felt into different shapes quickly and to assume the proper expression that fits the character you are impersonating. Practice will enable you to do the former and you can master the second by standing before a mirror and looking at yourself the while you are doing it.

As an example of the characters you can impersonate is the easy one of the cowboy, Alkali Ike, the Vatican guard, Pat and his piece o' pipe, George Washington, Napoleon, a soldier at Valley Forge, a Salvation Army lass, a heathen Chinee, the Pied Piper of Hamelin, Louis XV, etc.

A Marionette or Puppet Show.—What we call a *marionette* is a jointed doll or puppet that is made to move in a more or less lifelike manner by strings attached to it, which are manipulated by the hobbyist. To make a set of small marionette puppets and work them for your own pleasure or that of a few friends is the easiest thing you know, but to give a real marionette show you must have a set of properly made puppets dressed to fit the characters they are to play.

---

[12] You can make this of a piece of thick woolen goods, but one made for the purpose will give better results. A *felt* can be bought from any dealer in magical apparatus, or of the maker A. W. Gamage, Ltd., London, E. C. 1, England.

While you can buy the puppets ready-made, it is a wonderfully interesting hobby to make them yourself [13] and this I strongly advise you to do. To learn to work the puppets so that their actions will be as nearly true to life as it is humanly possible to make them, requires much skill and, hence, you will have to do a lot of practising, but in this also lies one of the chief interests of the hobbyist.

To give the show you must have a miniature stage with a proscenium and all of the equipment including curtains, scenery, properties, lighting, etc. Finally you must have a playlet for the puppets to give, and this you can write yourself, basing it on *Little Red Riding Hood,* or some other nursery tale.

A Second Sight Act.—*Second sight* is the transmission and reception of thoughts at a distance without the use of the physical senses. Whether there is really such a thing as second sight I wot not, but one thing I do wot and that is that every exhibition of it is not due to the mental transference of thoughts, but to various schemes that are a part of the magician's art.

Now there are two kinds of second sight acts and these are done by (*1*) the verbal system, and (*2*) the silent system. In the *verbal system* you transmit your thoughts to your assistant, or *subject* as he or she is called, by word of mouth, but in such a way that the spectators do not know it; while in the *silent system* you do not speak a single word.

The bald effect of the verbal second sight act is that you, as the *master mind,* i. e., the one who is sending out

[13] The way to make and work the puppets, and build the stage, is fully described in *The Amateur Entertainer*.

the thought waves, pass among the spectators; they hand you various small articles such as coins, pocket-pieces, knives, watches, rings, and the like, one at a time, and as you look them over your subject instantly describes them. This system employs certain key words as for example when you say, "Hurry, now, please tell me what this is," your subject translates it to mean that it is a copper penny and the date on it is 1933.[14]

In the silent second sight system, the effect, insofar as the spectators are concerned, is exactly like that of the verbal system, but the mystery of it is mightily enhanced because there is not a single word spoken on your part. There are several systems by which this can be done; thus Robert Heller, half a century or more ago, used a regular telegraph apparatus; Harry Kellar, a quarter of a century ago, used a concealed telescope and a speaking tube, and the present writer devised one that is worked by wireless telephony. This latter system is at once easy to do, certain in its operation, and very mystifying to the spectators.[15]

The Calostro Mind-Reading Act.—This is by all odds the finest, newest and most puzzling of all the second sight acts yet devised, for questions that are merely whis-pered into the ear of the master mind, i. e., the performer, are instantly answered in detail by his blindfolded assist-ant. The blindfold is genuine, there is no mechanical or electrical apparatus used, and the master mind never speaks a word to his assistant.

[14] You will find the verbal system described in detail in *The Book of Magic* as well as Heller's and Kellar's silent second system.
[15] You will find my silent second sight system fully explained in *The Amateur Entertainer,* as well as a phase of mental magic.

The resultant effect is just as uncanny and impenetrable as though it was accomplished by real mind-reading. This amazing act was invented by my lifelong friend, Ralph W. Read, for professional mind readers, but it is equally suitable as a hobby for the amateur mentalist. The complete system is described by Mr. Read in a sealed book which is sold at *$10.00* a copy, and you can get one of the *Calostro Publications,* P. O. Box *76,* Times Square, New York City.

The Art of Mind-Reading.—The hobby that goes by the name of *mind-reading* is an art by which you can indicate, in a rather roundabout fashion, a thought that is in a person's mind. The person, or *subject,* as he is called, can be a stranger to you, and neither of you speak a word except for the instructions you give him as to the method of procedure.

The effect of the following mind-reading test will suffice for all of them for they are done in exactly the same way. You let some one blindfold you and then ask the subject to hide a pin, while two or three others watch you to be sure you do not peek and see where he conceals it. The subject can hide the pin anywhere he wants to—under the lapel of some spectator's coat, the cuff of his trouser leg, the edge of a rug, the seat of a chair, or wherever it may please his fancy to do so.

Having hidden the pin at some little distance from you, you ask the subject to return, then to hold your *right wrist* with his *right hand,* as shown in *Fig. 70,* and to concentrate his mind on where he has hidden it. You then start off on a dead run pulling the subject along with you. The moment you reach the approximate place where the pin is hidden you begin an intensive search for it by feeling around, when you will speedily find it, to the amazement of the subject as well as the spectators.

The way you read his mind is this: You have him con-

FIG. 70.—A MIND-READING EXHIBITION

centrate it on the place where he has hidden the pin, and you make your mind as void as you can, except to the sensation of the *feel* of his hand that is holding your wrist. Now when you start off on a run with him he will *involuntarily* pull this way and that on your wrist and so lead you to the pin. Then when you get close to it his hand will give a perceptible jump; this is your cue that you have located it and by feeling around a little you will easily find it.

From this you will see that mind-reading is really *muscle reading,* for you do not find the pin by reading his mind, but by the muscular twitching of his hand. There are quite a number of tests in mind-reading that you can do, but while they differ one from the other, all of them are based on the principle of the pin test. The effects of the various tests, the way to do them, and the patter that goes with each one, are all given in detail in my *Book of Magic.*

Animal Magnetism and Hypnotism.—*Animal magnetism* is an alleged force that is supposed to be inherent in the human body, and to emanate from the extremities of it, just as ordinary magnetism is inherent in a steel magnet and to emanate from its poles. *Hypnotism* is alleged to be a condition that resembles sleep and this is supposed to be produced in a subject by the force of animal magnetism. When in this imaginary state, the subject is supposed to act upon and to carry out any suggestion that the so-called hypnotist makes to him, all of which I declare is the rarest kind of bunk, and I will not withdraw my affidavit.

To give you an idea of the numerous weird and wonderful things that you can do—not with animal magnetism, because it is non-existent, but in the name of it— here are a few of them that you can show: (*1*) You lay a lead pencil in the open palm of your hand and make it rise to a vertical position and then lie down again, and this without physical contact, at least as far as the spectators can see; (*2*) you show a large, hollow, brass ball and make it float in the air; to show that it remains

suspended without being supported in any way you pass
a hoop over and around it, as shown at *A* in *Fig. 71,* and
(3) you duplicate the inexplicable tests [16] of *Anna Abbot,*
the *Little Georgia Magnet.*

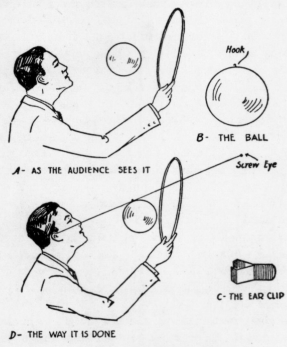

A- AS THE AUDIENCE SEES IT

B- THE BALL

Screw Eye

C- THE EAR CLIP

D- THE WAY IT IS DONE

FIG. 71.—A BALL FLOATING IN THE AIR

Having demonstrated the effects of animal magnetism
on inanimate matter, you proceed to show the effects of
it on animate matter, and this you do by hypnotizing a

[16] They may be *inexplicable* but I have explained them all, together
with the preceding tests in animal magnetism and those which follow in
hypnotism in my book, *The Amateur Entertainer.*

subject. By making passes over his face and body you induce the first three degrees, or states, of hypnotism, or you say you do, and these are (*1*) the lethargic, (*2*) the comatose, and (*3*) the cataleptic degrees.

In the *lethargic degree* the subject is not asleep but he

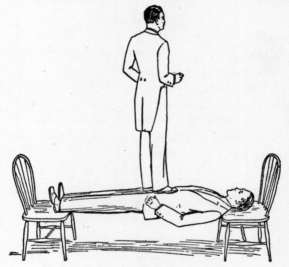

FIG. 72.—ANIMAL MAGNETISM AND HYPNOTISM

has not the power to move a single muscle of his body; in the *comatose degree* he is to all intents asleep but he will respond to any suggestion you may make him and, finally, in the *cataleptic degree* his muscles become as rigid as though *rigor mortis* had set in.

When in this latter state his body is as stiff as a stiff— I mean a cadaver—and you can then with the help of an assistant, place him with his head on one chair and his feet on the other, his body thus forming a bridge between them. While in this position you can stand on him, as pictured in *Fig. 72,* and still he remains the essence of rigidity itself.

After this awe-inspiring test, you and your assistant can lift him off of the chairs and again stand him on his feet. To de-hypnotize him you simply snap your fingers near his ear, when he will slowly come back to earth; his muscles gradually relax, he will open his eyes and he is, apparently, none the worse for wear.

A Spiritualistic Séance.—Of all the blood-curdling, nerve-racking and marrow-congealing hobbies that I know of, the *spiritualistic séance* takes the blue ribbon. I don't mean that the above adjectives apply to you as the gentle medium who acts as the connective between this world and the next, but to the spectators who behold Little Eva and your Indian guide, Chief Red Feather, do their stuff.

Now there are two general kinds of spiritualistic séances, i. e. where the tests take place, (*1*) in full light, and (*2*) in the cabinet. Of those *in the light* are such tests as spirit slate writing, bowl and table lifting, and table rapping. Those *in the cabinet* are of two kinds, (*a*) physical tests, and (*b*) materialization phenomena.

Physical tests include the ringing of bells, the banging of tambourines and the blowing of horns, action at a distance without physical contact, and other impossible feats. *Fig. 73* gives a faint idea of a séance of this kind. *Materialization phenomena* consist of producing the spirit form of a beautiful girl who has been given the celestial name of *Etherea.*

After you have materialized *Etherea* out of the fourth dimension, she floats gracefully into the air and remains

there for a time without any visible means of support—
in which respect she is not very different from a lot of
us poor mortals here below. At your command she gyrates

FIG. 73.—A SPIRITUALISTIC SÉANCE

and goes through other evolutions in thin air and then
returns to the cabinet.

The luminous stuff of which she is made grows smaller
and beautifully less until, finally, she has completely de-
materialized and returned to her spiritual haunts—probably Child's restaurant across the street. The way to
make the cabinet, to have yourself securely tied in it,
perform the physical tests, materialize and dematerialize
Etherea, and the pat patter that you can use when you
do the act are all explained in detail in my *Book of Magic.*

CHAPTER XII

SOME SCIENTIFIC HOBBIES

IF you would know the secrets of nature, insofar as they are knowable at the present time, if you would rise above the level of the average intelligent person of today, or if you like the study of science for its own sake and to experiment with scientific things, then you should move into the same stall with some one of the hobbies described in this chapter. While each one of the following hobbies requires intensive thought and seriousness of purpose, you do not need to be afraid to ride it, for all you have to do is to begin at the very bottom and then climb on up and into the saddle by easy steps.

The Hobby of Astronomy.—*Astronomy* is the science which treats of the heavenly bodies, of their sizes, motions, distances, what they are made of, etc., and there is no finer hobby in the whole category of those that are given in this book than this basic one whose field is the universe. Now the hobby of astronomy consists chiefly of observing the heavenly bodies, and while you can do this with your naked eye, you can add mightily to the pleasure and interest of it by using a telescope.

The Hobby of Star Observing.—By *star observing* I mean looking carefully at everything that you can see in the sky, and this includes the fixed stars, the blazing sun, the bright planets, the pale moon, the fiery comets, the burning meteors, etc. To start off the hobby of star observing all you need is a pair of good, sharp eyes and a clear space from which you can see as much of the sky as possible.

Naked-Eye Observing.—The first thing to do in making astronomy your hobby is to learn the *constellations*, as the various groups of fixed stars are called. Even if you don't know any of them, a glance at the sky on a clear night will show you that a large number of the stars form definite figures. For example, if you will look at the northern sky you will see *Ursa Major*, or the Great Bear, but which is usually called the *Big Dipper*, because it has the shape of one. Opposite to it is *Cassiopeia*, the Lady in the Chair, but which has the form of the letter *W*. The North Star, *Polaris*, is midway between these two constellations.

Then as you look along toward the south a little you will see *Andromeda*, the Lady Chained to the Rock; *Perseus*, the Hero; *Auriga*, the Shepherd; *Lyra*, the Lyre; *Cygnus*, the Swan; *Hercules*, the Strong Man; the *Great Square* of *Pegasus*, the Winged Horse; *Canis Minor*, the Little Dog, and a few other smaller constellations. Farther south, along the apparent path of the sun, or *ecliptic*, as it is called, you will see the twelve constellations of the *zodiac* beginning with *Pisces*, the Fishes, and ending with *Aquarius*, the Water Bearer. Finally, you will see *Orion*, the Mighty Hunter, which is, by a long shot, the most striking constellation in the whole heavens; *Hydra*, the Water Snake, *Ophiuchus*, the Snake Charmer, *Cetus*, the Whale, and numerous other southern constellations.

You will also see quite a number of first magnitude,

colored, variable, and a few double stars, and also the planets in all their glory. By looking at the sun through a piece of colored or smoked glass, you can just barely see the large spots on it; also a large dark oval spot on the moon; the *Great Nebulæ* of Orion and Andromeda, comets, meteors, and many other things.

Opera Glass Observing.—By using an *opera glass*, or still better, a *field glass*, for observing, the fixed stars will show up brighter, and you can see more of them than with your naked eye. Turn your glass on *Cassiopeia* and the five bright stars that look like the letter *W* will burst like a skyrocket into a myriad of stars. Then look at *Cygnus*, in the Milky Way, and you will see a galaxy of stars the like of which you never dreamed. Turn your glass on *Vega*, a first magnitude star in Lyra, and you will see a double star called *Epsilon* very close to it.

The most interesting object in Andromeda is the *Great Nebulæ;* in *Hercules*, the famous star cluster, known to astronomers as *13 M*, the *Pleiades* in Taurus, the *Ass's Colts* and *Manger* in Cancer, the *Great Nebulæ* in Orion, the giant star *Betelgeuze* also in Orion, etc. Having observed these, direct your glass on any of the planets and you will see that they are disk-shaped whereas the fixed stars always show as mere points of light. If you have sharp eyes and a good glass, you may be able to see one of the moons of Jupiter. You can also see the spots on the sun and the mountains on the moon quite clearly.

Observing with the Telescope.—To observe the heavens to the best advantage the telescope's the thing. With a *3*-inch refracting telescope,[1] or a *6*-inch reflecting tele-

[1] The way that this is made is described and pictured in my book, *Experimental Optics*, published by D. Appleton-Century Co., New York.

scope you can see a little star called *Sidus Ludovicianum* between the double star, *Mizar* and *Alcor* in the handle of the Big Dipper; *Albireo*, a double, and *Omicron*, a quadruple, in Cygnus. The double *Eta* in Perseus, and the quadruple *Epsilon* in Lyra; *Castor,* one of the twins [2] in Gemini, is an easy double to resolve with your telescope, and *Beta* a double, and the star clusters, *4M, 6M* and *7M,* in Scorpio. Then there is the temporary star, *1604* in Ophiuchus, and the binary star, that is a double the components of which revolve around each other; *Gemina* in Virgo, and many other doubles, triples and quadruples can be clearly separated.

There are also numerous nebulæ and star clusters, the phases of Mercury and Venus, Mars, that looms up like a fiery red ball, the four larger moons of Jupiter, the rings of Saturn; and the distant planet Uranus can also be sighted. With your telescope you can see not only the mountains on the moon but the crater rings, the dead seas, gulfs and plains. Naturally, the spots on the sun can be seen to greater advantage with a telescope than with an opera glass, and it also follows that the larger your telescope is the greater resolving power it will have.

How to Begin.—The first thing to do when you have made up your mind to take up astronomy as a hobby is to get a book on it that tells in simple language about the fixed stars, the constellations, the sun, planets, moon and various phenomena of the heavens. Either my *Book of the Stars,*[3] or *The Boy Astronomer,*[4] will tell you just

---

[2] The other twin star is *Pollux.*
[3] Published by D. Appleton-Century Company, N. Y.
[4] Published by the Lothrop, Lee and Shepard Company, Boston.

what you should know in the beginning about these things.

Having read up on the subject the next thing to do is to go out on a clear night and pick out the various

FIG. 74.—THE BARRITT-SERVISS STAR AND PLANET FINDER

constellations. An easy way to do this is get a little paper that is published for the amateur called *The Monthly Evening Sky Map*.[5] This gives an evening and a morning sky map for each month, and all you have to do is to hold the map over your head and you will see the stars

---

[5] This is published by Leon Barritt, 244 Adams Street, Brooklyn, N. Y. The subscription price is only $1.50 a year.

and planets in exactly the same positions that they are in the sky.

Another easy and most interesting way is to get a Barritt-Serviss *Star and Planet Finder,* which is pictured in *Fig. 74.* With this little instrument you can find any constellation or planet you want, at any hour of the day or night, time of the year, and for any year past, present and future. This is also sold by Leon Barritt, and the price is *$1.50.*

The Hobby of Telescope Making.—Making your own telescope is a hobby in itself and while it properly comes under the head of the manual arts, I have put it in here because it is so closely allied with observing. Amateur telescope making has a tremendous following both in the United States and in England at the present time, and it is one of the finest hobbies imaginable to pursue indoors when winter comes. But first off the thing for you to do is to get acquainted with the starry heavens, and then you will have a better idea of what you want in the way of a telescope.

Now there are two kinds of astronomical telescopes and these are, (*1*) refracting telescopes, and (*2*) reflecting telescopes. A *refracting telescope* is one that has two lenses in it, namely, an object-glass, or *objective* as it is called, and an eye-lens, or *ocular,* as shown at *A* in *Fig. 75.* A *reflecting telescope* has an eye-lens, but instead of an object-glass it has a *concave mirror* to gather in the rays of light from the object that is being observed, as at *B.*

While it is not an easy thing for the average amateur to make an object-glass that will give the necessary definition and freedom from aberration, it is, on the other hand, a comparatively easy matter to make a concave mirror that will be accurate enough for all ordinary purposes. This is the reason that the great majority of amateur telescope makers prefer to construct reflecting telescopes.

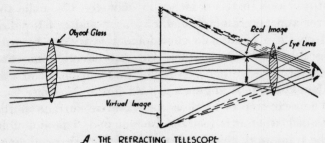

A THE REFRACTING TELESCOPE

FIG. 75A.—A REFRACTING TELESCOPE

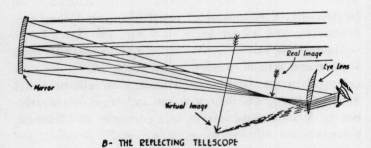

B- THE REFLECTING TELESCOPE

FIG. 75B.—A REFLECTING TELESCOPE

How to Begin.—I cannot give you here all of the constructional details for making a reflecting telescope, but I'll do the next best thing and tell something about it and where to get the necessary information and materials. The three chief parts of a reflecting telescope are

(*1*) the concave, silvered-glass mirror, (*2*) the ocular or eye-lens and (*3*) the mounting for them.

If you are a beginner in the noble hobby of telescope making, you should try your prowess on a small mirror first, say one that is *6* inches in diameter. To make the mirror you take a blank disk of glass [6] and grind, polish and give it a paraboloid curve, and this you do by rubbing the disk with another one and having some fine grains of abrasive between them. You can do all of this by hand, and it is not such a hard job to do either.

The next step is to silver the concave surface of the glass disk when it is ready to be mounted. The mounting is the framework that holds the reflecting mirror and the eyepiece in position, and you can make it of wood, pipe-fittings, discarded motor parts, and the like. It is better to buy the eyepiece, since it is quite inexpensive and hard to make, as it is formed of two convergent lenses, i. e., a field lens and an eye lens.[7]

Having the various parts, all that remains to be done is to assemble them, when your telescope, which will have cost you in the neighborhood of *$25.00*, will be worth about *$250.00*, and you will get an astronomical value out of it in star education and pleasure of *$2,500.00*, more or less.

Before you start to make a telescope you should get a copy of *Amateur Telescope Making,* published by the Scientific American, *24* West *40*th Street, New York City. The price of it is *$3.00* and it contains detailed informa-

[6] You can get blank disks, eyepieces, mountings, and complete kits of the Tinsley Laboratories, *3,017* Wheeler Street, Berkeley, Calif. Write them for their illustrated catalogue.

[7] You can buy these of Carl Zeiss, Inc., *485* Fifth Avenue, New York City, or of Bausch and Lomb, Rochester, N. Y.

tion on every phase of making reflecting telescopes, a list of books on making them, a list of professional and amateur astronomical societies with their addresses, a list of periodicals for the amateur astronomer, a directory of amateur and professional workers, and last, and most important of all, a list of the materials you need, together with beginner's kits, and the addresses of the dealers who sell them.

The Hobby of Microscopy.—A *microscope* is, as you probably know, an optical instrument that consists of a combination of lenses for making enlarged or magnified images of minute objects. *Microscopy* (pronounced mi-*kros'*-co-pe) is the use of, or investigation with, a microscope, and a *microscopist* (pronounced mi-*kros'*-co-pist) is one who uses a microscope.

Astronomy is a hobby that has to do with exceedingly large and infinitely distant objects of the universe, whereas microscopy is a hobby of the exceedingly minute and often invisible objects that are immediately at hand. And while astronomy is essentially an out-of-door hobby, microscopy is strictly an indoor hobby.

How to Begin.—Having decided to take up microscopy as a hobby, the first thing to do is to get a microscope, and this can be an inexpensive one that magnifies the objects you are observing from *75* to *300* diameters,[8] depending on the power of the eyepiece you use; the cheapest one will cost you in the neighborhood of *$15.00,* and this is the *New Gem* microscope, see *Fig. 76,* that is made by the Bausch and Lomb Optical Co., of Rochester, New York.[9]

---

[8] The powers at which most amateurs and many professional microscopists work are between *75X* and *300X*.

[9] Write them for a detailed description of it and also for a catalogue

Now there are two chief kinds of objects that you can examine with a microscope, namely, (*1*) those formed of inanimate matter, which is matter that has never lived, and this includes the rocks, minerals and metals, and (*2*)

Fig. 76.—An Inexpensive Compound Microscope

animate matter, that is, matter that is living, or which has once lived, as the plants and animals.

In beginning your hobby you can investigate and examine objects of every kind, such as fabrics, paper, foodstuffs, as the starches, the sugars, tea, coffee, and animal foods, and preservatives, adulterants, drinking water, etc. After you know how to make observations with your

and price list of their other and better microscopes. Carl Zeiss, Inc., *485* Fifth Ave., N. Y., also make a very fine line of microscopes.

microscope, you must learn how to dissect, mount and stain the minute objects so that you can see them to the best advantage. To do these things you will need (*1*) some dissecting tools, and (*2*) a dissecting microscope, and both of these are very inexpensive.

Then you must get some mounting materials and these include (*a*) glass slides and cover slides, and (*b*) glycerine, albumen or balsam, for mounting the object on the slide. You will find clear and simple descriptions of all of these things and how to mount the specimens in my *Book of the Microscope.*[10]

When you have learned a little about dissecting an object and mounting the minute parts of it on a slide, you can cut the gizzard out of a cricket or a beetle, the salivary glands out of crickets and cockroaches, the stings out of bees and wasps, and other like operations too numerous to mention.

After You Get Started.—While it is most interesting to take a look at various minute objects through a microscope, still, to make a real hobby of it, you should take up the study of *Botany;* then beginning with the lowest forms of plant life, one of which is the *algæ,* or *frog-spittal* as it is often, but wrongly, called, you can go on up the scale until you come to the highest forms which are the *Angiosperms,* or family of flowering plants.

When you have made a systematic examination of the plants, you should take up the study of *zoölogy,* and beginning with the lowest forms of animal life, which is the single-celled animals, such as the *amœba* of the rhizopodic protozoan family, go on up the scale until you come

[10] Published by D. Appleton-Century Company, New York.

to the highest forms which are the *vertebrata*, or animals with backbones.

If after you have made a study of the elementary characteristics of plant and animal life, you and your hobby are still going strong, then you can take up any of the highly specialized branches such as *physiology*, which deals with the processes, activities and phenomena of life and living organisms; *histology*, which deals with the tissues in their normal conditions; *morphology*, which deals with the forms and structure of plants and animals; *cytology* which deals with the individual cell and its characteristics and functions; *bacteriology*, which deals with bacteria, etc.[11]

When you have mastered one of these studies with the aid of your microscope you will probably have metamorphosed from the hobbyist class into the professional class, and your services may be worth anywhere from *$1,500* to *$10,000* a year, depending on how expert you are.

[11] For textbooks on these subjects, write the Macmillan Co., the McGraw-Hill Publishing Co., and the John Wiley Co., all of New York City.

CHAPTER XIII

SOME MORE SCIENTIFIC HOBBIES

The Hobby of Chemistry.—*Chemistry* is that branch of science that has to do with the composition of substances and of the transformations which they undergo when they react on one another. Now there is no scientific hobby that you can take up which will give you a greater insight into the workings of Nature than chemistry, and provide you with more pleasure than to make various substances combine and produce other and entirely different substances. Moreover, many of these reactions set up very remarkable and exceedingly spectacular effects, all of which are highly interesting, entertaining and instructive.

How to Begin.—There are three chief parts to chemistry: (*1*) the theoretical, that is, the principles it is based on, (*2*) the experimental, wherein you get certain results by trial, and (*3*) the practical, which has to do with its useful applications. Your interest in chemistry as a hobby will be confined chiefly to the experimental part of it, but to get the most pleasure and benefit out of it, you must know what takes place and why it does so when a reaction is going on.

Now there are two ways to start to ride the hobby of chemistry, and these are (*1*) to buy a *chemical outfit,*[1]

[1] Chemicraft Set. A. C. Gilbert, Fales Chemical Co., Cornwall Landing, N. Y.

which includes the chemicals and apparatus for performing a certain number of experiments, and (2) to buy the
chemicals and apparatus [2] you need for the particular
experiments you want to do. If you are a boy or a girl,
the best way for you to start is to buy one of the chemical
outfits, see *Fig. 77,* and these can be had in various sizes,

FIG. 77.—EXPERIMENTING WITH CHEMISTRY

for performing a small or a large number of experiments,
and at prices ranging from *$1.00* to *$15.00.*

If you are a man or a woman and want to take up
chemistry as a serious hobby, then the better way is for
you to buy the chemicals and apparatus as you need
them. Assuming that you are going to do it this latter

[2] You can get these of The Central Scientific Co., *460* East Ohio Street,
Chicago, Ill., or of Eimer and Amend, *18*th Street and Third Ave., New
York City.

way, you must of necessity have a book that will tell you how to make the experiments and you will find a very complete list of them, which are arranged in the proper sequence, in my *Experimental Chemistry*.[3]

While this book gives you the *cause why* of the reactions that take place for each experiment, so that you will have a glimmering of what it is all about, still you will profit greatly by reading carefully my other book called *How to Understand Chemistry*,[3] as this gives you the theory of chemistry in language you can easily understand.

When you have made the experiments described in the first mentioned book and carefully digested the contents of the second one, you will have an understanding of chemistry beyond that of a high-school student and you will be ready to matriculate for a college course in chemistry.

The Hobby of Electricity.—This is one of the hardest ridden hobbies of all of those that come under the general head of science. All over this fair country of ours, and I dare say, other civilized countries as well, you will find a table or a bench in the basement, the kitchen, the bedroom, in the attic, or out in the barn or the garage, that is littered with wire, fixtures, apparatus and tools; here old as well as young experimenters spend their spare time playing with batteries, bells, telegraph and telephone sets, electric lights, dynamos and motors, while many of them are more seriously at work on inventions of one kind or another that have to do with electricity, or in which electricity has to do with them.

How to Begin.—There are numerous ways to start

[3] Published by D. Appleton-Century Co., N. Y.

electricity off on a trot, and if you dig your spur in deep enough, you will soon have it running for all it is worth on a fast track and making a mad dash down the home stretch. The way that lots of experimenters mount the hobby of electricity (see *Fig. 78*), is to buy a few dry cells, some insulated wire, a couple of miniature lamps,

FIG. 78.—MAKING ELECTRICAL EXPERIMENTS

a toy motor, a screwdriver and a pair of pliers—and this soon leads to other pieces of apparatus and tools.

There are, however, so many and diversified branches of electricity that it is by far the better way to choose some one of them and then ride it to the finish. Thus you can specialize in telegraphy, telephony, motors, electroplating, high-frequency electricity, radio, etc. Whichever one you take up you should by all means make all of the apparatus you can, for this is not only an interesting hobby in itself but it will give you a wonderful insight into the whys and wherefores of electricity.

If you want to make batteries, electro-magnets, a Morse telegraph, a Bell telephone, a spark-coil, a dynamo or motor, do electric wiring, measure electricity and learn the basic principles of the electric current, read my *Book of Electricity*. If, however, you are more interested in making electrical experiments than in the apparatus itself then get my book *Fun with Electricity*.[4] The last named book explains how to perform a large number of striking experiments with alternating current as well as with direct current, and complete instructions are given for making and using high-frequency apparatus.

You can get the materials to build all of the things described in these books at any electrical supply house, or if you live in the wide open spaces where there aren't any, then send to the *Central Scientific Company*, Chicago, Illinois, tell them just what you want, and they will quote you prices.

The Hobby of Radio.—*Radio* is the foal of Old Man-o'-War *Electricity*, and they are running a neck-to-neck race for a sweepstakes. Experimenting with radio—especially short-wave radio—is the one best bet for first place on the program today. It is not at all an expensive hobby, takes up a small amount of room, and oh, boy, what a kick you will get out of the set you build when you pull in Rabât, Morocco, or Nairobi, Africa, and other DX stuff from half-way 'round the world.

How to Begin.—The logical way to start the hobby of radio is to build some kind of a simple receiver first. Now

---

[4] Both of these books are published by D. Appleton-Century Company, N. Y.

while there are lots of books on radio—I have written
several myself—the advances in the art come along so
fast that they are out of date almost before they come
off of the press. It is the radio papers that carry the last
word in the design and construction of receivers, and these
are on the news-stands in every town and city in the United
States and Canada. Better than to buy these by the month,
is to subscribe for one or more of them by the year.

Fig. 79.—A One-Tube Short-Wave Radio Receiver

The first receiver you build should be a simple one
and any number of these have been published at different
times in the aforesaid papers, and new ones are appear-
ing all the time. As I am writing this I have before me
a copy of *Radio News* [5] for September, *1934*, and on

---

[5] The makers and dealers of the various parts that are used are advertised in the paper and you can get their catalogues and price lists for the
asking.

page *150* there is a complete description, together with all of the parts that are needed, for a one-tube, *short-wave receiver* which was made by Robert Crockett, a Boy Scout, of Pelham, New Jersey. This is pictured in *Fig. 79*.

It has a circuit that was made famous by the above named paper in *1928*, called the *junk-box circuit*, and it has been built by hundreds of radio hobbyists who have found it highly successful for receiving over long distances. You can get a complete set of full-scale blue-prints that show you exactly how to wire up the different components, as the parts are called, for *25* cents. With this set you can log the British, Spanish, French and German short-wave stations and, of course, all of the powerful ones on the American continents.

After you have built and used this short-wave receiver, you will have a very good idea of how to build an *all-wave receiver,* or any other kind that you may care to. You will also probably have some ideas of your own and you can then work out new circuits and arrangements and, perhaps, hit upon something that will be of real value to the art of radio.

The Hobby of Television.—*Television* is the art of *seeing by electricity* and this may be done over wires, or without wires, that is by means of radio-waves. There are several short-wave television sending stations on the air in various cities, and hundreds of hobbyists, who have built their own receivers, receive the images they send out. To build a simple television receiver is not any harder than to build a broadcast receiver, and as it is the coming thing you should get in on it now.

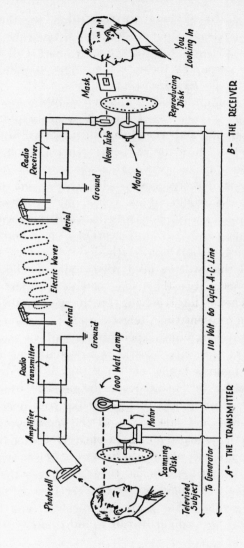

Photocell

Amplifier

Radio Transmitter

Aerial

Ground

1000 Watt Lamp

Electric Waves

Aerial

Radio Receiver

Ground

Neon Tube

Mask

Reproducing Disk

You Looking In

Motor

Scanning Disk

Televised Subject

Motor

To Generator

110 Volt 60 Cycle A·C· Line

A — THE TRANSMITTER

B — THE RECEIVER

FIG. 80.—AN EXPERIMENTAL TELEVISION APPARATUS

How to Begin.—There are several different schemes by which television can be done, but the two chief ones are by (*1*) the scanning disk and (*2*) the cathode-ray tube. The easiest way to begin the hobby of television is to get my book *Experimental Television.*[6] It tells how both the scanning disk and cathode-ray tube transmitters and receivers are made and work. A simple experimental television sending and receiving outfit is shown in *Fig. 80.*

You can buy all of the parts for either a scanning disk or a cathode-ray receiver and assemble them yourself. The scanning disk receiver is the easiest and cheapest to make and I would advise you to build one of these first so that you will get clearly in mind the theory and requirements of television reception. You should then tackle the job of building a cathode-ray receiver, for this is the kind that will be used when television becomes a household necessity—that is if some one doesn't get up a better scheme for receiving the images in the meantime. At the present time, television offers the most fruitful field of research and experimental work of any of the branches of electricity, and as it is bound to come you had better make a hobby of it and play it to win.

The Hobby of Home Recording.—The term *home recording* means, simply, that you make your own phonograph records, and this is one of the most entertaining hobbies in the whole realm of science. Not only this, but you can make records of the voices of your kiddies as they are growing up, and file them along with the snapshots you take of them, in which case they will have a deep sentimental value.

Now what we ordinarily call sound is a wave motion

[6] Published by Lothrop, Lee and Shepard Co., Boston, Mass.

in and of the air, and audible sound waves, i. e., those that you can hear, can be set up by anything that vibrates between the limits of *14* and, say, *20,000* times per second. To record these waves, you must make them operate a stylus, or needle, as it is commonly called, and this cuts a spiral groove in a rotating disk of some suitable material.

To reproduce the recorded sound waves you need only to place a reproducing needle in the spiral groove that the recording needle has cut, and then rotate the disk at the same speed it revolved at when you were making the record. Both the recording and reproducing operations are, of course, done with the aid of the phonograph.

Methods of Recording.—There are two ways by which you can make the sound waves set up by your own or some one's else voice, a musical instrument or other vibrating body, operate the recording or cutting needle and so cut the variable groove in the record blank; these are, by speaking (*1*) into the mouthpiece on whose diaphragm is fixed the cutting needle, and (*2*) into a microphone which is connected with an electromagnetic pickup through an amplifier.

The first way is quite simple, and with it you can record voice sounds by talking or singing very closely to the mouthpiece, as shown at *A* in *Fig. 81*. The disadvantage of this method is that since the force of the sound waves alone must make the diaphragm vibrate, the movements of the needle, which is fixed to it, are so slight the groove it cuts in the blank record is not very deep and, it follows, the reproduction will not be very strong.

The second and more satisfactory way to record

voices, music, etc., is to connect a microphone to a three-tube amplifier, and this to the electromagnetic pickup of your phonograph, as pictured at *B;* or if you want to record a song, or anything else that you get on your radio,

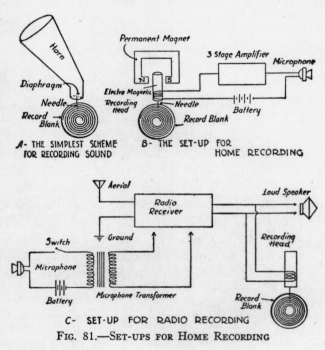

A- THE SIMPLEST SCHEME FOR RECORDING SOUND

B- THE SET-UP FOR HOME RECORDING

C- SET-UP FOR RADIO RECORDING

FIG. 81.—SET-UPS FOR HOME RECORDING

you have only to connect the output terminals of the transformer that leads to the loud speaker to the pickup as at *C*.

How to Begin.—To begin the hobby of home recording you need *(1)* a turn-table, *(2)* a pickup, *(3)* a level indicator, *(4)* an amplifier, *(5)* a microphone, *(6)* a microphone transformer, (7) some blank recording disks, and (8) some recording and reproducing needles. The turn-table consists of a rotatable disk, upon which the record blank is laid that is to be cut, and this is run by a motor that drives a rubber friction pulley, a rubber coupling, or a belt.[7]

The electromagnetic pickup is formed of a combined permanent and electromagnet with a cushioned pivoted armature between its poles, and in the lower end of it (the armature) is a cutting head which has a set-screw in it, and this holds the cutting needle as shown at A in Fig. 82 A and B.

A level indicator is, simply, a vacuum tube voltmeter and this operates on the principle of a vacuum tube detector. Now while the usual practice is to test the cutting level of the needle by the feel of it with your fingers, or by means of a monitor microphone, the level indicator gives by far more accurate results, and to do a really good job of recording it is a necessity.

A recording amplifier should have at least three stages of resistance-coupled tubes, see B, and these should be high-gain, audio-amplifier ones. The microphone should be of the double carbon button type, while the microphone transformer consists of a primary and a secondary coil wound on a soft iron core.

The blank disks on which the records are cut are made of various materials, the chief ones being gelatine, celluloid, aluminum and a composition called duralotone. For experimental home records gelatine blanks will do well enough. They have the advantages of being cheap,

[7] In other words, when you are making a record the turn-table should not be rigidly connected to the motor by metal gears.

and practically free from background noise. You can buy
gelatine in sheets *20* inches on the sides for *30* cents a

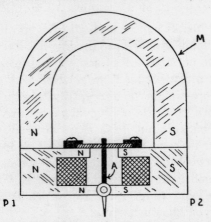

A— HOW THE ELECTROMAGNETIC PICK-UP IS MADE

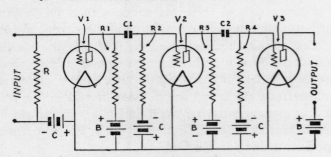

B— THREE STAGE RESISTANCE COUPLED AMPLIFIER

FIG. 82.—THE ELECTROMAGNETIC PICKUP AND AMPLIFIER UNIT

sheet.[8] Its disadvantages are numerous, and chief among
these are (*a*) that the pickup must have a feed-screw for

[8] These are sold by the Charles Products Co., *78* Cliff St., New York
City.

cutting the spiral line, (b) the water in the gelatine tends to dry out when the record will get brittle and chip and crack.

Celluloid blanks can be had with the spiral uncut, that is without being grooved, or pregrooved. If you use the latter you do not need a feed-screw for cutting the groove. Celluloid is much harder than gelatine and, hence, there must be more weight on the cutting needle and, it follows, a more powerful motor must be used. There is, also, more background noise than with gelatine records but this can be reduced by rubbing oil or vaseline on it. There are two kinds of celluloid and these are (a) the acetate, which is non-inflammable, and this is what you want to use, and (b) the nitrate, which is inflammable, and which you should not use.

The aluminum blanks can be had either ungrooved or pregrooved, and these are made with a highly polished surface; the surface of it should be either waxed or oiled to fill the pores and to lubricate the needle. Finally, the duralotone blanks [9] have a soft surface which permits it to be cut easily with a steel needle and to record perfectly the sound waves. After recording, the disk must be permanently hardened and this you can do by simply heating it in an ordinary oven, or in an oven especially made for the purpose.

When the record is so treated it looks like an ordinary bought record and will outlast it. It has a metal base and will not break if it should happen to fall; it is lighter in weight and thinner than a standard record, and it can be played on any standard phonograph.

[9] Duralotone disks and all other home recording apparatus can be had of the Sound Apparatus Co., 150 West 46th St., New York City.

The recording needles are made of steel or of an alloy of chromium-steel [10] and the cutting ends of them are ground like those of metal cutting lathe tools. When you are cutting gelatine blanks you should use a sharp, flat-bottomed needle. For cutting celluloid, aluminum and duralotone blanks, a sharp, diamond-pointed needle gives the best results. For playback, that is reproducing the recorded sounds, you should not use steel needles, as these wear the sound track away very quickly, and so fiber and thorn needles are employed, and these must be kept very sharp.

Before you take up home recording as a hobby you should by all means read a little book called *Home Recording and All About It*, which is a very good treatise for the beginner. It was written by George J. Saliba, and is published by the *Gernsback Publications, Inc., 98 Park Place, New York City.*

The Hobby of Weather Forecasting.—What we call the weather is a state or a condition of the atmosphere, i. e., whether it is hot or cold, wet or dry, calm or stormy, clear or cloudy, etc. Now there are two ways to forecast the weather, and these are by (*1*) ancient proverbs which are often in rhyme, and (*2*) with the aid of meteorological instruments. The first named are but little better than blind guesses, while the second are based on scientific facts.

The Barometer.—The chief instrument that is used for forecasting the weather is the barometer and it is used to determine the weight, or the pressure, of the atmosphere, which amounts to the same thing, and it is the

[10] These are made by the RCA Victor Co., Inc., Camden, N. J.

variations of this factor that are chiefly responsible for good, bad, and indifferent weather.

There are two chief kinds of barometers and these are (1) the mercurial barometer and (2) the aneroid [11] barometer. The mercurial barometer consists of a graduated glass tube about 34 inches long and this is filled with mercury; the tube is then inverted in a cup that contains mercury. The column of mercury falls until its weight is exactly balanced by that of the atmosphere, and its rise and fall is a measure of the change in the weight and, it follows, pressure of the air.

The aneroid barometer, which is shown in *Fig. 83*, works on a very different principle from that of the mercurial barometer, in that the atmospheric pressure bends the thin corrugated top of a closed and partially exhausted box and this moves a needle or hand over a graduated scale. The aneroid barometer is not as accurate as the mercurial barometer but as it is very compact and easily carried it is the kind you want at least for your initial experiments.

How to Read the Barometer.—The indicating hand of the barometer, which is usually blue, points out any change in the pressure of the atmosphere and, it follows, any change in the existing weather conditions. A checking hand, which is light colored, can be turned by a brass knob outside of the glass; by setting this hand in alignment with the blue hand, it is easy to follow any change in the position of the latter.

[11] This word is compounded from the Greek letter *a* which means *not* and *heros* meaning *moist* or *wet*, i. e., containing no liquid, plus the combining form, *oid*, from *eidos* meaning *like*.

Now all barometers that are intended for home weather forecasting are marked *Rain, Change* and *Fair*, and sometimes *Stormy* and *Very Dry*. When the hand points to *Fair*, it means that the weather will be *Fair* over a certain area and for a given length of time. When it points to *Rain*, it means that there may be showers, rains, thunderstorms, or snow, depending on the locality and the season. But you must not pin your faith on the

Fig. 83.—An Aneroid Barometer for Forecasting the Weather

words *Fair* and *Rain* that are marked on the dial but to the barometer rising and barometer falling.

Barometer Rising.—(1) A gradual and steady rise indicates that the weather will be fair and settled; (2) a very slow rise from a low point indicates that high winds and dry weather will prevail, and (3) a rapid rise indicates that clear weather and high winds are likely.

Barometer Falling.—(1) A gradual but steady fall indicates unsettled or wet weather; (2) a very slow fall from a high point indicates that the weather will be wet and unpleasant, and with little wind, and, finally,

(3) a swift fall indicates a sudden shower, or high winds, or both.

How to Start.—To become an amateur meteorologist [12] (pronounced me-te-or-*ol'*-o-jist), you should get *(1)* a good aneroid barometer, and *(2)* a book on weather forecasting. The aneroid barometer, and all of the others that have to do with meteorology, are made by the *Taylor Instrument Co.*, Rochester, New York. You can get an aneroid barometer for about *$10.00*, or a better one called a *Semi-Automatic Indicator*, or *Stormograph* as it is called, for about *$20.00*. This latter instrument is an aneroid barometer, but its dial is so arranged and worded that it makes it easy for you to instantly forecast the weather.

A very good little booklet for you to start with is *Practical Hints for Amateur Weather Forecasters*, written by P. R. Jameson, F.R.M.S., F.R.G.S. and published by the Taylor Instrument Co. This company also publishes a number of other booklets on weather forecasting, the price of each one of which is *15* cents, except one called *Weather and Weather Instruments*, which costs *$1.00*.[13]

[12] A meteorologist is one who specializes in the phenomena of atmosphere or weather.

[13] You can get the above instruments and booklets of Pickup & Brown, Inc., opticians, *580* Fifth Avenue, New York City.

INDEX

289

(5)